Preface

Chinese in Steps is a series of textbooks designed for English-speaking adults who learn Chinese either as part of their degree programme at university, or as part of their professional or self-development study. The series aims to develop learners' productive communicative competence by focusing on key generic speech patterns and making listening and speaking the core activities of each lesson. Reading and writing skills are also introduced step by step to enable the learners to understand and use Chinese effectively. This approach is based both on cognitive research on how English-speaking adults learn Chinese as well as our experience in teaching learners of Chinese as a foreign language. The layouts of the books is designed to make the contents easy to access and follow. Grammar explanations are given where necessary, but grammar jargon is kept to a minimum.

Chinese in Steps, as the name suggests, consists of steps set within several stages, and there are two volumes (steps) in each stage. The four books for the first two stages – Beginners and Lower Intermediate – are designed to cover most key speech patterns, fundamental grammatical knowledge and about 1000 most frequently used characters with over 2500 words, most of which are vocabularies used in everyday life. By the end of these two stages, learners should be able to cope with everyday life needs in a Chinese speaking environment. While aiming to deliver an effective and enriching experience in learning the Chinese language, the textbooks also take into consideration the needs of those who seek externally validated qualifications. The first four books are comparable to the current requirements of higher GCSE and up to AS level in the British education system, and to B1.1 level to the European Benchmarks for Chinese Language (EBCL) based upon Common European Framework for languages (CEFR).

Chinese in Steps Volume IV is the second book of the Lower Intermediate stage, (B1.1CEFR). It is recommended for those who have completed Volume III. Since it was published over ten years ago in 2008, a lot of changes have taken place in the daily life of the people in China and their use of everyday language. As China provides the background for the contents of this volume, there has been a clear awareness on the part of the authors of the need to update this volume to reflect the rapid changes in China as well as to better serve the needs of the users of this series of textbooks. This revised edition is very much the results of such awareness and the feedback that the users have kindly provided over the years.

This volume is designed to review major speech patterns covered in the first three volumes and to use the language in scenarios that learners are most likely to encounter in China. Like the three previous volumes, this book also contains 10 lessons, and each lesson still has two dialogues and a reading passage set in an everyday life scenario. The relevant language usages - particularly on the structure of Chinese vocabulary - are explained in the notes on grammar and within the exercises. Cultural notes remain, but an additional reading is now included at the end of each lesson, introducing a common Chinese proverb and its story. The learners can expect to encounter many of such proverbs as they continue with their study.

It is hoped that the users of the revised edition find not only the topics and vocabularies more up-to-date, but also find the exercises more user-friendly. We would like to take this opportunity to thank all the users who have kindly given us their feedback and we welcome further feedback, comments and suggestions for future editions. Finally, we would also like to thank the publisher, Cypress Book (UK) Ltd for their support.

George X Zhang
Linda M Li
William X Yu
Yi Yang

June 2019

CHINESE IN STEPS

STUDENT BOOK 4
步步高中文 4

George X Zhang

Linda M Li

William X Yu

Yi Yang

Sinolingua · London

Every effort has been made to trace all copyright holders, but if any have been inadvertently overlooked, the publisher will be pleased to make the necessary arrangements at the first opportunity.

Chinese in Steps Series
Chinese in Steps (Student Book 4)
By George X Zhang, Linda M Li, William X Yu, Yi Yang

Commissioning editor: Ranran Du, Chengqian Guo

Chinese editor: Ranran Du, Fenfen Bao

English proofreader: Rory Howard

Cover design: China-i

This new version, first published and Copyright © 2021 by Sinolingua London Ltd. is published under permission from Cypress Book Co., (UK) Ltd. The original version of Chinese in Steps Volume 4 (ISBN 9781845700249) was published by Cypress Book Co., (UK) Ltd. in 2009.

Unit 13, Park Royal Metro Centre
Britannia Way
London NW10 7PA
Tel: +44(0)2089611919
E-mail: editor@sinolingualondon.com
Website: www.sinolingua.com.cn

Distributed by Cypress Book Co., (UK) Ltd.
Tel: +44(0)2088481500
Fax: +44(0)2085611062
E-mail: sales@cypressbooks.com
Website: www.cypressbooks.com

Printed in the People's Republic of China

ISBN 978-1-907838-13-2

All rights reserved. No part of this publication may be reproduced or transmitted by any means, electronic, mechanical, photocopying or otherwise, without the prior permission of the publisher.

目 录 Contents

预备课	Warm-up Lesson	1
第三十一课	在学校注册	8
第三十二课	选修课	21
第三十三课	在银行	34
第三十四课	寄包裹	47
第三十五课	理发	61
第三十六课	请假	74
第三十七课	写信	87
第三十八课	申请工作	99
第三十九课	购物	113
第四十课	故宫	126

附 录 Appendices

1. 组词游戏	Word Game	138
2. 听力原文	Listening Scripts	139
3. 练习答案	Keys to the Exercises	152
4. 汉英词汇表	Chinese-English Vocabulary List	161
5. 英汉词汇表	English-Chinese Vocabulary List	182

语法术语简略表　Abbreviations of Grammatical Terms

adj	adjective	形容词
adv	adverb	副词
comp	complement	补语
conj	conjunction	连词
id	idiomatic expression	惯用语
int	interjection	感叹词
l.w	location word	方位词
m.v	modal verb	情态动词
m.w	measure word	量词
n	noun	名词
num	number	数词
o	object	宾语
pt	particle	助词
p.n	proper noun	专有名词
pron	pronoun	代词
prep	preposition	介词
q.w	question word	疑问词
s	subject	主语
t.w	time word	时间词
v	verb	动词
v-c	verb-complement	动补结构
v-o	verb-object	动宾结构

● Chinese characters noted with * are usually not used on their own, but as a component of a word.

预备课
Warm-up Lesson

Learning Objectives
This lesson revises the essential speech patterns and vocabulary covered in Book Three. It serves as a preparatory lesson for Book Four.

 对话1 Dialogue One

学生：师傅，我去北京语言大学。

师傅：好。你的行李这么多，小箱子放在大箱子上，可以吗？

学生：大箱子里面有瓶子，小心别把瓶子弄破了。

师傅：车后备箱恐怕装不下了。

学生：那把小箱子放在我旁边的座位上吧。

师傅：好。上车吧。

学生：谢谢。

师傅：你是来上学的吧？

学生：对，我来学一年中文。

师傅：你是哪国人？

学生：一下子说不清楚。我爸爸是法国人，我妈妈是德国人。

师傅：你是在哪儿出生的？

学生：德国。不过一岁时我就去了法国，我是在法国长大的。

师傅：你是在哪儿上的学？

学生：小学是在法国上的，中学和大学是在英国上的。

师傅：你拿的是哪国护照？

学生：我有两本护照，一本是法国的，一本是英国的。

Notes:
后备箱　hòubèixiāng　boot (car)
一下子　yíxiàzi　at one go (in a few words)
长　zhǎng　grow, grow up

师傅：那你只能说是欧洲人了。

学生：对，我是欧洲人，西欧人。

对话 2 Dialogue Two

Notes:
西欧　Xī'ōu　western Europe
交通　jiāotōng　traffic, communication
拥挤　yōngjǐ　crowded
班车　bānchē　service bus

学生：师傅，北京的交通总是这么拥挤吗？

师傅：今天还可以，有时候更拥挤。

学生：真没想到北京有这么多汽车，跟伦敦差不多。

师傅：现在有钱的人多了，有汽车的人也就多了。

学生：我听说中国是自行车的王国，上下班时人们都骑自行车。

师傅：那是过去。现在开车的、坐地铁的、坐公共汽车的、坐班车的、打的的、骑自行车的、什么样的都有。

学生：师傅，北京汽车进城要不要交进城费？

师傅：不用。听说伦敦进城要交五镑钱，是吗？

学生：现在涨了要交十一镑五了。

师傅：太多了！一天十多英镑，合人民币九十多块钱呢。

学生：多是多，可是现在开车上班的人少了，交通好多了。

师傅：出租车司机怎么办？他们天天在城里开车，也要交钱吗？

学生：好像他们不用交。

师傅：这还差不多。

Notes:
进城费　jìnchéngfèi　congestion charge (for driving into city)
合　hé　(colloquial) be equivalent to
这还差不多　That's probably reasonable

阅读 Reading

画儿是谁偷的？

张先生是个警察。这天晚上，他接到一个电话，听不清说话人的声音，只听到有人说："美术馆 (art gallery) 的名画儿被偷了。"他放下电话后马上去了美术馆。美术馆里有两个工作人员，一个是上早班的，一个是上晚班的。张先生问他们："是谁发现画儿被偷了？"上晚班的说："他刚才告诉我的。"张先生就问上早班的："你是什么时候发现画儿被偷走的？"上早班的说："就在刚才。我两个小时前关门的时候画儿还在。回家的路上我想起来有件东西忘在办公室了，所以又回来了。到了这儿以后，我发现画儿不见了。"这时张先生又问："你们认为 (think) 画儿是谁偷的呢？"上早班的人说："不知道是谁打的电话。他一定跟偷画儿的人有关系。"张先生说："你说得对。我知道是谁偷的了。"

问题：

1. 张先生怎么知道画儿被偷了？
2. 美术馆有几个工作人员？
3. 是谁最先发现画儿被偷了？
4. 他们什么时候发现画儿被偷了？
5. 上早班的工作人员为什么又回来了？
6. 你认为是谁偷的？

练习 Exercises

口语练习 Speaking Practice

1. 情景对话：两人一组，一人当出租汽车司机，一人当留学生，在对话中了解以下情况：

- 留学生是哪国人？学了多久的汉语？
- 留学生想不想住在当地人家里？
- 留学生想不想天天坐出租车去上学？
- 留学生想不想租车出去玩儿？他想去哪里玩儿？
- 出租车司机是老北京吗？他住在市中心吗？
- 出租车司机觉得他的收入怎么样？
- 北京的交通怎么样？北京的天气怎么样？
- 出租车司机有没有朋友的孩子想学英语？

2. 你坐飞机去北京，你和坐在你旁边的人交谈。你想知道：

- 他/她为什么去北京？
- 他/她要在北京住多久？他/她要住在哪儿？
- 他/她都打算在北京做什么？
- 他/她是不是自己一个人去北京？
- 他/她还打算去中国什么地方？

听力练习 Listening Practice

Listen to the following dialogues and choose the correct answer for each question.

1) a. 出租车上　　b. 机场里　　c. 汽车站里
2) a. 有人偷了　　b. 有人拿错了　　c. 我太累了
3) a. 我的中文书　　b. 我的护照　　c. 一件礼物

4) a. 又生气又着急　　b. 给警察打了电话　　c. 告诉了老师
5) a. 系里的老师　　　b. 看门的师傅　　　　c. 一个没见过的人
6) a. 护照上　　　　　b. 箱子里面　　　　　c. 行李卡上
7) a. 他没吃过西餐　　b. 饭很便宜　　　　　c. 他不要我的钱
8) a. 这位好司机　　　b. 司机的老板　　　　c. 饭店经理

语法练习 Grammar Practice

1. 多项选择

1) 请告诉我您打算星期几 ____ 中国去。
   a. 想　　　　　　b. 到　　　　　　c. 要

2) 旗袍看 ____ 很漂亮，可是大多数人穿不了，只有瘦人才能穿。
   a. 上来　　　　　b. 出来　　　　　c. 起来

3) 这个人非常聪明，什么东西都学得 ____。
   a. 下　　　　　　b. 过　　　　　　c. 了

4) 请你快把行李准备 ____，我们马上就走。
   a. 好　　　　　　b. 到　　　　　　c. 了

5) 你能不能写得清楚一点儿，我看不 ____ 这是什么。
   a. 好　　　　　　b. 懂　　　　　　c. 了

6) 她人 ____，可是很多人都喜欢她。
   a. 好看　　　　　b. 很好　　　　　c. 不漂亮

7) 这本书写得不 ____，没有人爱看。
   a. 好极了　　　　b. 怎么样　　　　c. 很不错

8) 你怎么连这么大的字都看不 ____？！
   a. 见　　　　　　b. 好　　　　　　c. 完

9) 这么多的饭我们吃不 ____，快给老王送一点儿去。
   a. 好　　　　　　b. 到　　　　　　c. 了

10) 她一边说，一边哭。没说几句就说不 ____ 了。
   a. 下去　　　　b. 下来　　　　c. 上来

2. 选词填空（有的词可重复使用）

着、了、得、就、过、正、到

花园里放 ____ 一张桌子，一只兔子 (tùzi) (rabbit) 和一个戴 ____ 大帽子的人 ____ 坐在桌子旁边喝茶。桌子下面躺 ____ 一只 ____ 在睡觉的老鼠 (lǎoshǔ) (mouse)。一只可爱的小松鼠 (sōngshǔ) (squirrel) ____ 靠 (kào) (to lean against) 在老鼠身上说话。桌子大 ____ 很，可是他们看 ____ 爱丽丝 (àilìsī) (Alice) 来了，____ 说："没有地方了，没有地方了！"爱丽丝说"地方多 ____ 很"，就在桌旁坐 ____ 下来。

兔子说："喝点儿酒吧。"可是桌子上只有茶，没有酒。爱丽丝说："我没喝 ____ 酒，不会喝。"

认字识词 Words with Known Characters

查找出下列词语的词义，并翻译成英文。

名词 _____	动词 _____
形容词 _____	副词 _____
代词 _____	专有名词 _____
数词 _____	量词 _____
介词 _____	连词 _____
感叹词 _____	象声词 _____

翻译练习 Translation

Say the following sentences in Chinese first and then write them out in characters.

1) May I leave my luggage here?
2) There are too many books and they can't fit into my bag.
3) How much does a ticket to Derby cost?
4) Can you help me pay for my drink first?
5) Transport is the biggest problem here.
6) The weather in Shanghai is quite similar to that of London.
7) Your luggage is too heavy and you can't take it onto the plane.
8) I am always very busy in December and don't even have time to visit my mother.
9) I didn't expect him to be over sixty years old because he looks as if he is in his forties.
10) I am afraid I will have to see your passport before I can give you the ticket.

CHINESE IN STEPS 4   Lesson 31

31
第三十一课　在学校注册

Learning Objectives
To register for a course/club
To understand about studying in China
To fill in a course application form in Chinese

🔊 生词 1 New Words

读	dú	动	read; study (a subject)
报到	bàodào	动	report one's arrival or presence
如果	rúguǒ	连	if 如 if
学位	xuéwèi	名	(academic) degree
中文系	zhōngwénxì	名	department of Chinese language and literature
进修	jìnxiū	动	engage in advanced studies 修 repair; study
注册	zhùcè	动/名	register 注 record, register 册 volume, book
录取	lùqǔ	动/名	admission; admit (on a programme) 取 get, take
通知书	tōngzhīshū	名	(information)letter, notification
李健	Lǐ Jiàn	专名	Li Jian, Jay Lee 健* healthy
有意思	yǒuyìsi	动/形	be interesting 意思 meaning 思 thought, think
起名	qǐmíng	动+名	to name, to give name to
力量	lìliàng	名	strength 量 capacity; quantity
表格	biǎogé	名	forms 格 square formed by cross lines; check
预订	yùdìng	动	book (a place, ticket etc.) in advance
办理	bànlǐ	动	deal with, process 办 do, handle
手续	shǒuxù	名	procedure 续 continue
办公室	bàngōngshì	名	office
交费	jiāofèi	动+名	pay fees
钥匙	yàoshi	名	keys 钥* key 匙* key; chí: spoon

对话1 Dialogue One

学生：请问，读中文的是在这儿报到吗？

老师：如果①你读学位，请到中文系报到。

学生：我不读学位，我是来进修的。

老师：那你找对地方了，进修的就是在这儿登记注册。

学生：谢谢！这是我的录取通知书和护照。

老师：你的英文名字叫Jay Lee，中文名字叫李健，很有意思。

学生：这个名字是我的中文老师给我起的，我很喜欢。

老师：不错，好记，意思也好，很有力量。请你填写一下这张表格。

学生：用中文填还是用英文填？

老师：如果你能用中文填，那就用中文填。

学生：好。老师，我还预订了留学生宿舍。

老师：办理完登记手续以后，到对面的办公室去交费取钥匙。

学生：谢谢。

生词 2 New Words

王小明	Wáng Xiǎomíng	专名	Wang Xiaoming
来自	láizì	动	come from
马来西亚	Mǎláixīyà	专名	Malaysia
理科	lǐkē	名	science (subjects of study) 科 branch; subject
数学	shùxué	名	maths 数 number
杂志	zázhì	名	magazine, journal 杂 mixed 志 records
阅览室	yuèlǎnshì	名	reading room 阅 read 览 browse
文科	wénkē	名	humanities
设备	shèbèi	名	facilities 设 set up
先进	xiānjìn	形	advanced
空调	kōngtiáo	名	air conditioner 调 adjust
不然	bùrán	连	otherwise, if not
学习	xuéxí	动/名	study
开设	kāishè	动	set up, offer
对外汉语	duìwài hànyǔ	名	Chinese as a foreign language
大量	dàliàng	形	a great quantity, a large number
零起点	língqǐdiǎn	名	ab initio; from scratch (starting from zero) 起点 starting point
为	wéi	动	be; become
进行	jìnxíng	动	conduct, carry out
会话	huìhuà	名	conversation
一般	yìbān	副/形	common; generally 般 type; like
每	měi	代	every, each
人数	rénshù	名	number of people
大约	dàyuē	副	approximately 约 about
清真	qīngzhēn	名	Islamic, Muslim
菜系	càixì	名	style of cooking, cuisine
校园	xiàoyuán	名	campus

补充词汇 Additional Vocabulary

化学	huàxué	chemistry	政治	zhèngzhì	politics
生物	shēngwù	biology	经济	jīngjì	economics
物理	wùlǐ	physics	教育	jiàoyù	education
地理	dìlǐ	geography	商务	shāngwù	business
心理	xīnlǐ	psychology	建筑	jiànzhù	construction, architecture
历史	lìshǐ	history	法律	fǎlǜ	law

对话 2 Dialogue Two

王小明：你好！我叫王小明，来自马来西亚。

李　健：你好！我叫李健，来自英国。

王小明：我就住在你对面，325号房间。

李　健：你也是来读语言的吗？

王小明：不是，我是来读理科的，我读数学。

李　健：你去过学校的图书馆没有？我想去借本杂志看看。

王小明：学校有文科和理科两个图书馆。我只去过理科图书馆。

李　健：图书馆的设备怎么样？

王小明：很先进，有很多计算机，还有空调。

李　健：阅览室大不大？

王小明：很大。不过人很多，你要早去，不然就没有座位了②。

李　健：真的？！那我得走了。回头见。

王小明：回头见。

课文 Text

去中国学习汉语

如果你想去中国学习汉语,你要先找好学校。中国很多的大学都开设对外汉语课,有的在中文系,有的在语言中心。每年都有大量的外国留学生到中国的大学学习汉语。

开始上课以前,你要参加分班考试。初级班为零起点,一点儿汉语都不会的学生也可以参加。中级班的学生需要认识八百到一千多个汉字,能用汉语进行会话。高级班的学生需要认识一千五百多个汉字,能读懂中文报纸。每个班人数一般在二十人左右。

中国的大学一般上午八点开始上课,十二点吃午饭,中午休息两个小时,下午两点又开始上课。每周上课的时间大约为二十个小时左右。中国的大学一年分为两个学期,每年的九月初和二月底开学。每个学期的学习时间为十六到二十周。学校一般都有好几个餐厅,在那里你可以吃到来自中国不同菜系的饭菜,有的学校还有清真饭菜和西餐。中国大学的校园里一般都有留学生宿舍,宿舍里面有电视、空调和冰箱等设备,留学生大多喜欢住在留学生宿舍。

语法注释 Grammar Notes

①如果 – if. 如果 is formal, 要是 is informal (in Lesson 22, Book 3. While such conditional conjunctions are used in Chinese, they are often omitted if the relationship is clear from the context.

For example:
(1)(如果)你不去,我也不去。 If you don't go, I'm not going either.
(2)(如果)他能做好,谁都能做好。 If he can do it, anyone can.

However, if the condition relates to a past subjunctive, the conjunction 如果 is normally included.

For example:

(3) 如果你早点开始学，现在汉语应该说得很流利了。
If you'd started studying earlier, you would have been fluent by now.

(4) 如果他们昨天都来帮忙，这工作今天就该做完了。
If they had come to help yesterday, the work would have been finished today.

②不然就没有座位了 – "Otherwise there is no seat left." 不然 is the same as 不然的话 meaning "otherwise". Both expressions are commonly used in spoken Chinese. 了 suggests an imminent change of the state.

For example:

(1) 你快走吧，不然就晚了。
Go quickly, otherwise you'll be late.

(2) 你应该休息两天。不然的话，你会累病的。
You'd better rest for a couple of days, otherwise you'll get ill with tiredness.

文化知识 Cultural Note

中国大学的学期

An academic year for most of the higher education establishments in China consists of about 40 calendar weeks, which are usually divided into two semesters running from early September to January, with a break of 3 or 4 weeks for the Chinese New Year, then from February to early July, followed by about 8 weeks' summer vacation. Unlike in the UK, there is no half term or reading week during the semester in Chinese universities, but you have instead a midterm examination. It is common to have more than 20 contact hours of teaching per week. In terms of assessment, there is less course work but more formal examinations in Chinese universities than in the UK.

练习 Exercises

口语练习 Speaking Practice

1. 角色扮演

a. 你是一名新生，在校园里遇见了一个学生。你想知道他的个人情况和学校宿舍、图书馆、餐厅等情况。

b. 你是一名老生，你给A介绍你个人和学校的情况。

听力练习 Listening Practice

Listen to the following dialogues and choose the correct answer for each question.

1) a. 法国　　　　　b. 美国　　　　　　c. 英国
2) a. 游览北京　　　b. 在图书馆学习　　c. 在家里玩电脑
3) a. 月票　　　　　b. 录取通知书　　　c. 书包
4) a. 丢了　　　　　b. 没有收到　　　　c. 被朋友拿走了
5) a. 学费　　　　　b. 护照　　　　　　c. 简历
6) a. 中文系　　　　b. 音乐系　　　　　c. 数学系
7) a. 不给他注册　　b. 查找他的名字　　c. 打电话给他的朋友
8) a. 回家　　　　　b. 去找录取通知书　c. 去交钱

语法练习 Grammar Practice

1. 多项选择

1) ＿＿＿＿我明年去中国，我一定去找你。

　　a. 不然　　　　　　b. 如果　　　　　　　c. 因为

2) 我很幸运，我被上海大学＿＿＿＿了。

   a. 报到   b. 通知   c. 录取

3) 我们学校语言中心的设备很＿＿＿。

   a. 先进   b. 新鲜   c. 好极了

4) 请问，在哪儿＿＿＿住宿手续？

   a. 办理   b. 注册   c. 写

5) 李健＿＿＿一个医生家庭。

   a. 出来   b. 是   c. 来自

6) 我还没有拿到学位，＿＿＿这个工作就是我的了。

   a. 不但   b. 不然   c. 不是

7) 房子是＿＿＿人住的，你把房子空着，房子也会坏的。

   a. 需要   b. 不要   c. 一定

8) 在中国，对着门的座位＿＿＿上座。

   a. 办   b. 让   c. 为

2. 选词填空

可以、报到、和、读、考试、如果、
一起、参加、大约、然后

  如果你来我们学院＿＿＿学位的话，本科要读四年。申请人要有高中以上学历，汉语水平＿＿＿(HSK) 成绩要达到五级以上。你将和中国的本科学生＿＿＿上课，不过你可以少选几门选修课。＿＿＿你是交换生，你的学分可以转换。

  如果你来我们学院进修的话，你学习一到两年都＿＿＿。你要先到我们的对外汉语系＿＿＿，在那里学习汉语＿＿＿中国文化。学生注册后要参加考试，＿＿＿分班学习。对外汉语系共有四种班，入门 (entry level) 班、初级班、中级班和高级班，每班＿＿＿有十五到二十人。学习期间，学生可以＿＿＿汉语水平考试。

CHINESE IN STEPS 4   *Lesson 31*

认字识词 Words with Known Characters

1. 查找出下列词语的词义，并翻译成英文。

总数	_____	注意	_____
画册	_____	杂物	_____
思想	_____	游览	_____
阅读	_____	比如	_____
修理	_____	学科	_____

2. 翻译下列词语，并找出其结构规律。请至少再找出五个同样结构的词。

老汉	_____	老虎	_____
老公	_____	老婆	_____
老大	_____	老小	_____
小吃	_____	小费	_____
小店	_____	小菜	_____
小人书	_____	小朋友	_____

翻译练习 Translation

Say the following sentences in Chinese first and then write them out in characters.

1) The reading room at the British Library does not have an air conditioner.
2) Shall we meet at the coffee shop opposite my office at 12 tomorrow?
3) I can't find your name. Have you booked a room?
4) Students who are going to study Chinese please go to the second floor to register.
5) I am from Vietnam; he is from Mali.
6) You must pay the accommodation fee first, otherwise you can't have the key.

阅读 Reading

成语故事 The stories behind Chinese idioms

井底之蛙

一只青蛙(qīng wā)(frog)住在一口井(jǐng)(well)里。它高兴时就在井里跳来跳去，天热了就在水中游上游下，觉得很快乐。它想，我这里又大又舒服，哪儿也比不上我的井！

一天，青蛙在井边遇见了一只从海里来的大海龟(hǎiguī)(turtle)。青蛙就对海龟说："你看，我住在这里多快乐！你为什么不下来玩玩儿呢？"海龟听了青蛙的话，倒真想进去看看，可是它太大了，进不去。海龟只好趴(pā)(lie on one's stomach)在井口上对青蛙说："青蛙老弟，你见过大海吗？"青蛙说："大海比我的井大吗，海龟老兄(lǎoxiōng)(elder brother)？"海龟就把大海有多大、多深、多广都跟青蛙讲了。青蛙这才知道，井外还有这么大的天地。

实用练习 Module Practice

护照用名	姓			照 片
	名			
国 籍		出生地点		
出生日期	年　　月　　日		男 ☐	
			女 ☐	
已婚 ☐ 未婚 ☐	护照号码		宗教信仰	
最后学历			现职业	
现工作单位				
永久通讯地址				
电话　　　　传真　　　　　　电子邮箱				
目前通讯地址				
电话　　　　传真　　　　　　电子邮箱				
申请学习时间	从　　年　月　日 到　　年　月　日			
现有汉语水平（词汇量） Ⓐ 无　　Ⓑ 大约800　　Ⓒ 大约1500　　Ⓓ 大约2500　　Ⓔ 大约3500				
学生本人签字 日期				

汉字笔顺 Stroke Order

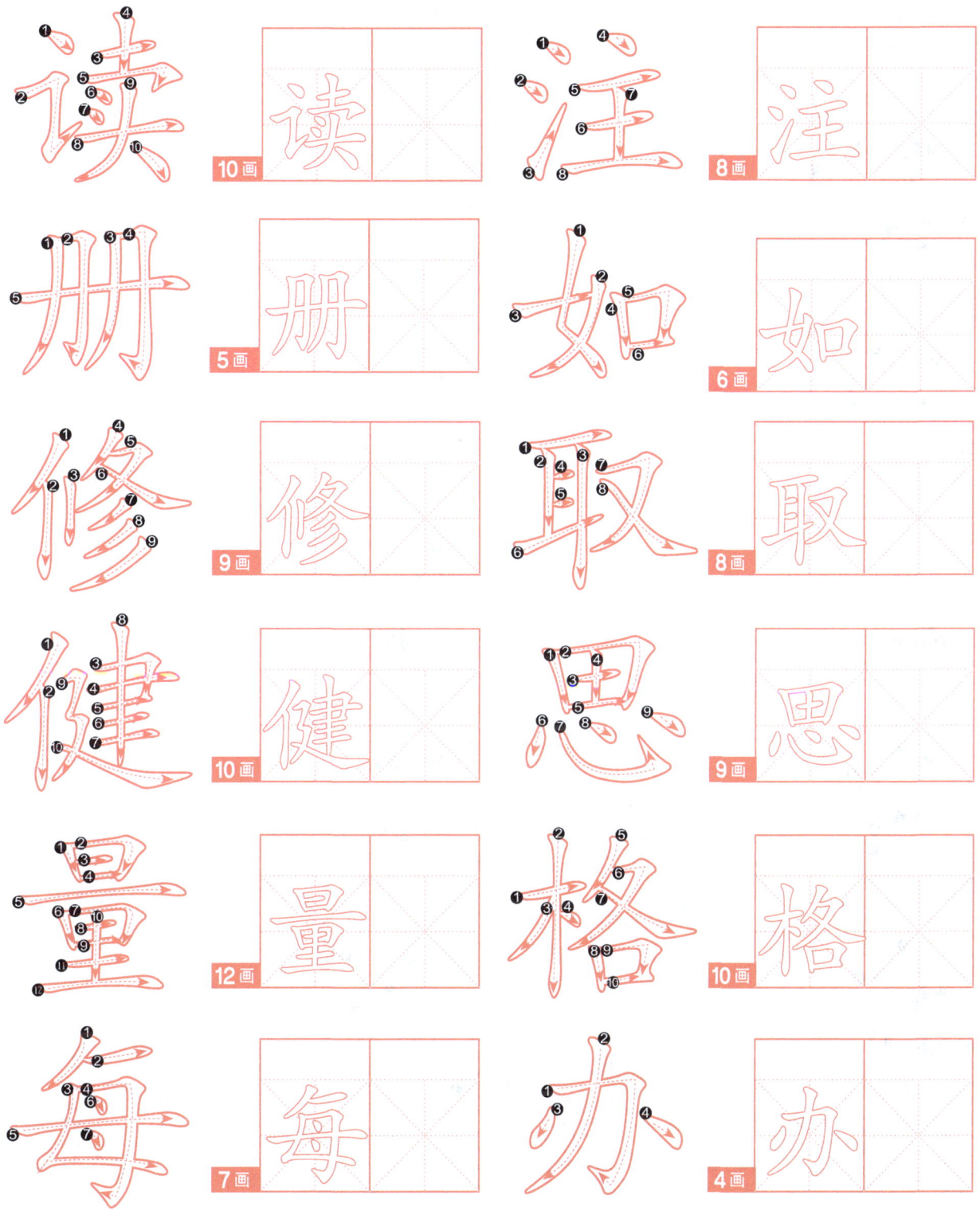

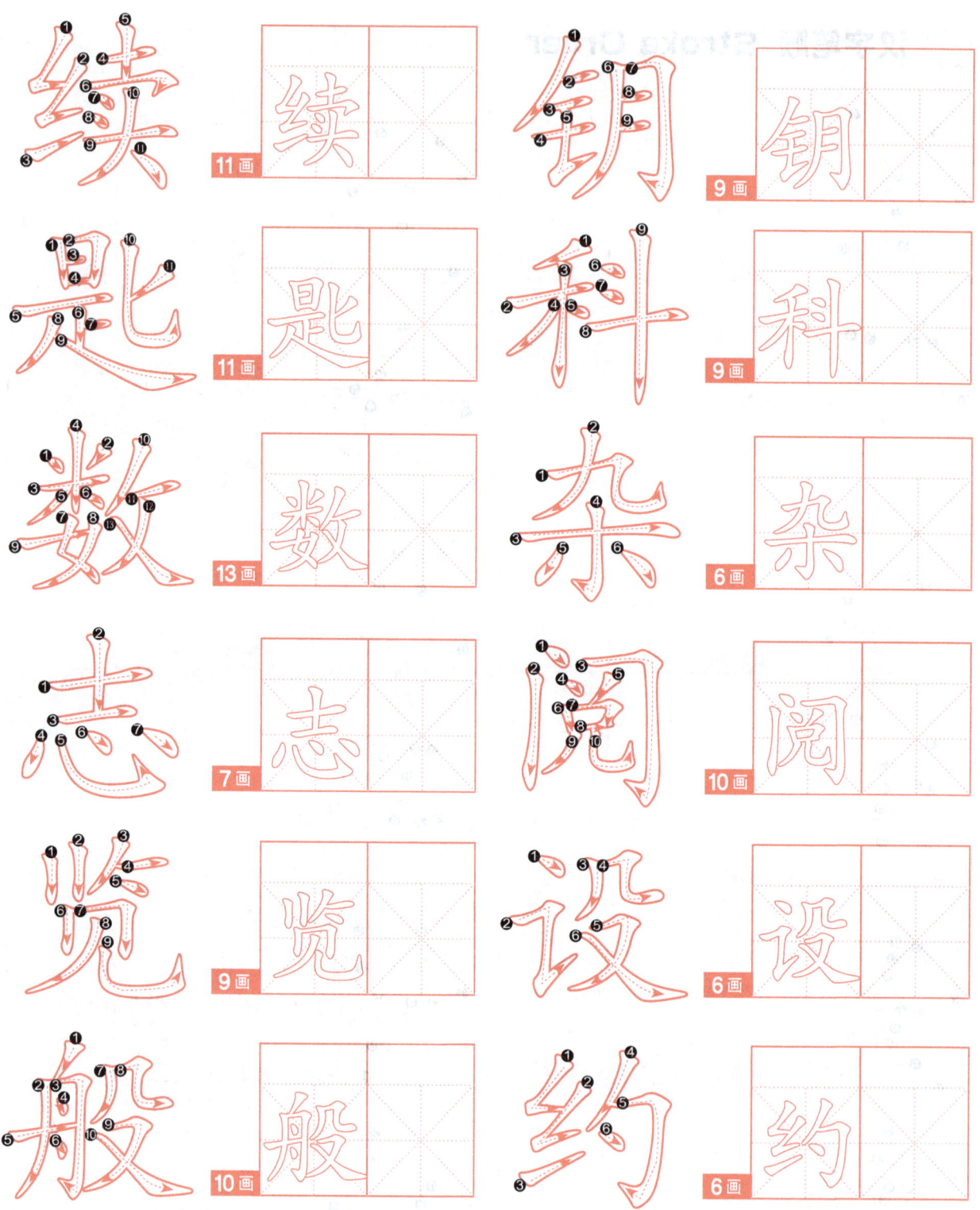

32
第三十二课　选修课

Learning Objectives
To make choices: the course to take or a club to join
To offer a reasoned explanation for your choice
To know about exercise and health in China

生词 1 New Words

词	拼音	词性	意思
选修	xuǎnxiū	动/名	select an optional course 选 select
目录	mùlù	名	list, catalogue 目 list; eye
武术	wǔshù	名	martial arts 武 military 术 art, technique
学名	xuémíng	名	scientific name, formal name
乒乓球	pīngpāngqiú	名	table tennis 乒* 乓* onomatopoeic characters
活动	huódòng	动/名	exercise; activity 活 live; alive
校队	xiàoduì	名	school/college team 队 team
队员	duìyuán	名	team member
私人	sīrén	形	private, personal 私 private, personal
教练	jiàoliàn	名	coach, trainer
商量	shāngliang	动	discuss, consult
门	mén	量	M.W for a school subject or area of study
学生证	xuéshēngzhèng	名	student card 证 certificate, card; proof
自动	zìdòng	形	automatic
方便	fāngbiàn	形	convenient

对话 1 Dialogue One

小李：您好！我想选修中国功夫课，可是目录上没有。

老师：有，你看，在这儿。

小李：功夫就是武术吗？

老师：对，武术是学名。

小李：我明白了，谢谢。

老师：武术课一周一次，星期二下午三点到四点。

小李：星期二下午我有乒乓球活动。

老师：这么巧。你是校队队员吗？

小李：不是。我刚刚开始学，请了个私人教练。

老师：那你跟教练商量一下，看看能不能<u>换个时间</u>①。

小李：好。我从小就喜欢中国功夫，我一定要选修这门课。

老师：那你可以现在注册。你带学生证了吗？

小李：我的学生证还没有办好，我还没拍照片呢。

老师：大厅里就有自动照相机，瞧，就在那边！

小李：我看到了，真是太方便了！我现在就去拍。谢谢！

老师：不客气！

🔊 生词 2 New Words

死	sǐ	形/动	to death (intensifier: "tired to death"); dead, die
节	jié	量	period, session
大部分	dàbùfen	名	most 部 department, part, section
迟到	chídào	动	arrive late 迟 late
不好意思	bùhǎoyìsi	短语	embarrassed; sorry
自觉	zìjué	形	conscious
书法	shūfǎ	名	calligraphy
健身房	jiànshēnfáng	名	gym 健身 keep fit 身 body
俱乐部	jùlèbù	名	club 俱 all, complete
锻炼	duànliàn	动/名	take physical exercise 锻 forge 炼 refine
不仅	bùjǐn	连	not only 仅 only
而且	érqiě	连	and; but also 而 but 且 and; just
不仅……而且……			not only…but also…
棒	bàng	名/形	bat, stick; terrific (colloquial)
棒球	bàngqiú	名	baseball
广场	guǎngchǎng	名	(city) square
身体	shēntǐ	名	body 体 body
重要	zhòngyào	形	important
年青人	niánqīng rén	名	young people
聊天	liáotiān	动	chat 聊 chat
会员卡	huìyuán kǎ	名	membership card 卡 card
改变	gǎibiàn	动	change 改 change, correct
方式	fāngshì	名	manner; approach

🔊 补充词汇 Additional Vocabulary

体育馆	tǐyùguǎn	sports hall, stadium	会员费	huìyuánfèi	membership fee
壁球	bìqiú	squash	跑步机	pǎobùjī	treadmill
保龄球	bǎolíngqiú	bowling	划船器	huáchuánqì	rowing machine
手球	shǒuqiú	hand ball	哑铃	yǎlíng	dumbbell

板球	bǎnqiú	cricket	运动会	yùndònghuì	sports game
球拍	qiúpāi	bat	奥林匹克	Àolínpǐkè	Olympics

对话 2 Dialogue Two

小方：小李，我快要累死了②，每周要上18节课。

小李：那我就更不用活了③，我要上22节，而且大部分都在上午。

小方：我的也是。天天早上8点就有课。

小李：我已经迟到两次了，真有点不好意思。

小方：问题是这里迟到的人很少，大家都很自觉。

小李：你还选修了别的课吗？

小方：选了，中国书法和太极拳。你呢？

小李：我参加了健身俱乐部，下午我要去健身房锻炼。

小方：学校里有健身房吗？

小李：不仅有，而且④很棒。

小方：真的？我还以为中国人只喜欢打乒乓球呢。

小李：他们什么球都喜欢。

小方：是吗？他们好像不喜欢打棒球。

小李：不是不喜欢，而是⑤没有场地。

课文 Text

新的生活方式

现在在中国，健身非常流行。男女老少都很喜欢健身。老年人一般都喜欢慢跑、打太极拳和跳广场舞。在城市里，每天早上你都会看到很多老人到公园去，先慢跑几分钟，然后打打太极拳。夏天的晚上，他们常常来到广场，和朋友们一起跳舞锻炼身体。他们都认为开始锻炼以后，身体比以前棒多了。现在锻炼成了他们生活中重要的一部分。

最近几年来，在大城市里到处都可以见到健身房。健身房里有各种健身设备，年青人都很喜欢去健身房锻炼。锻炼完以后可以在那里和朋友见面，喝杯咖啡，聊聊天。越来越多的年青人都办理了健身房的会员卡。有的人认为健身只是为了锻炼身体，可是有的人认为健身不仅仅是为了锻炼身体，健身还可以改变一个人的生活方式。这是一种新的生活方式。

语法注释 Grammar Notes

①换个时间 – "Change to another time." An expression often used when the time offered is not suitable. Please note the use of 个.

②我快要累死了。– "I am almost tired to death." 死 here means "extremely", and it usually follows an adjective to form a colloquial expression of "adj + 死 + 了".

For example:
(1) 这两天事情很多，我们都快忙死了。
There's been a lot to do this past couple of days; we've been rushed off our feet.
(2) 饭做好了没有，我都快饿死了。
Is dinner ready? I'm starving to death.

③那我就更不用活了。– "Well, my situation is even worse." (literally, it means: "In that case, I have even less chance to survive"). Please note the use of 更 (even more).

④不仅……而且…… – "not only... but also". However, 不仅 here is the same as 不但 and it is usually used together with 还, 也, 又. 不仅 can be omitted.

> **For example:**
> (1) 我不仅要选修武术，而且还要选修书法。
> I not only want to take martial arts, but also calligraphy.
> (2) 王老师（不仅）歌唱得好，而且舞也跳得好。
> Mrs Wang not only sings very well, but also dances well too.

⑤不是……，而是…… – "it is not... , but...". The expression is usually used to correct an erroneous impression or belief.

> **For example:**
> (1) 他不是不能来，而是不想来。
> It's not that he can't come but that he doesn't want to come.
> (2) 我不是不想唱，而是真的不会唱。
> It's not that I'm not willing to sing but that I really can't sing.

文化知识 Cultural Note

中国人的健身活动

Physical exercise is part of the Chinese way of life, though it takes many different forms. Many state institutions still hold annual competitive sports events. For ordinary people, the most popular forms of exercise are strolling, jogging, *tai chi and Qigong*. You will see these activities taking place all around you if you are in an urban area of China. Over the last twenty years, dancing (both Chinese and Western) has gained enormous popularity in urban areas, especially amongst retired people. For young professionals, gyms and sports clubs seem to be their favourites. In some metropolitan cities, paid gym or health club membership cards are among most favoured gifts for young people.

练习 Exercises

口语练习 Speaking Practice

1. 小组活动：一人当学校健身房注册员，其他人提问问题，例如健身房的设施、时间、费用等。
2. 小组活动：每人介绍一下自己最喜欢的运动。

听力练习 Listening Practice

Listen to the following dialogues and choose the correct answer for each question.

1)	a.机场	b.酒吧	c.舞会
2)	a.医生	b.工程师	c.教师
3)	a.音乐	b.数学	c.商务
4)	a.出了事故	b.太累了	c.没有学生
5)	a.今天晚上	b.明天晚上	c.后天晚上
6)	a.踢足球	b.打乒乓球	c.打篮球
7)	a.姚明	b.李明	c.姚英
8)	a.当教练	b.当老师	c.打篮球
9)	a.2 米	b.2.06 米	c.2.26 米
10)	a.3 号	b.13 号	c.30 号

语法练习 Grammar Practice

1. 多项选择

1) 今天晚上我们开会____一下下周的活动，好不好？
  a.选修　　　　b.商量　　　　c.做
2) 王先生是我的____马术教练。
  a.锻炼　　　　b.私自　　　　c.私人

3) 狗子是他的小名，他的____叫贵生。
   a. 学名   b. 姓名   c. 真名

4) 他____会打羽毛球，而且还会打棒球。
   a. 不是   b. 不仅   c. 不喜欢

5) ____意思，我今天又迟到了。
   a. 不好   b. 真有   c. 没有

6) 如果我不在家，我家的电话会_____转 (transfer) 到我的手机上。
   a. 自行   b. 应该   c. 自动

7) 你想____我，我还想改变你呢！
   a. 改变   b. 变化   c. 修改

8) 我家附近没有地铁站，进城很不_____。
   a. 快   b. 方便   c. 便宜

2. 选词填空

感觉、种、滑草、差不多、蓝、绿、
就像、那儿、人们、一开始

北京附近有好几个滑草场 (grass-boarding field)，夏天你可以去___滑草健身。滑草场的经理说，来滑草的有三____人：一种人是滑雪爱好者，到了夏天没有地方去，就来_____；另一种人不敢 (dare) 滑雪，就来滑草，试试滑雪是什么____；还有一种人就是喜欢户外 (outdoor) 运动的人，他们喜欢滑草场的___天____草。滑草跟滑雪_____，要穿滑草器，也要用滑草杖。滑草____和走路差不多，慢慢滑起来_____滑雪一样，可以滑得很快。____可以在山坡上滑，也可以在平地上滑。

认字识词 Words with Known Characters

1. 查找出下列词语的词义，并翻译成英文。

选美 _____	干活 _____
私自 _____	自私 _____
武打 _____	目前 _____
活鱼 _____	死人 _____
队长 _____	证人 _____

2. 翻译下列词语，并找出其结构规律。请至少再找出五个同样结构的词。

房子 _____	演员 _____
脑子 _____	卫生员 _____
篮子 _____	警卫员 _____
读者 _____	科学家 _____
记者 _____	歌唱家 _____
作者 _____	数学家 _____

翻译练习 Translation

Say the following sentences in Chinese first and then write them out in characters.

1) He was late again yesterday, but he did not seem to feel embarrassed at all.
2) My girlfriend has not only started to go to the gym every day, but she has also hired a personal trainer.
3) Table tennis is a very popular sport in China, most universities have a team.
4) It is not that he did not want to eat, but that he couldn't eat because of his illness.
5) Chinese calligraphy is very beautiful but seems difficult to learn. Do you think I can learn it?
6) When can we register for the kung fu class? I have been interested in this since childhood.

阅读 Reading

成语故事 The stories behind Chinese idioms

bá　miáo zhù zhǎng
拔 (pull) 苗 助 长

　　从前有一个农夫 (farmer)，种 (plant) 了稻苗 (rice seedling) 以后希望能早早收成 (harvest)，因此每天跑到稻田 (rice paddy) 去看。

　　每次到了稻田以后，他都发现稻苗长得非常慢，几乎没有什么变化。他心想："怎样才能让稻苗长得又快又高呢？"他想了又想，最后终于想出一个好方法，就是把稻苗拔高一点儿。

　　他忙活 (work hard) 了好几天，终于把稻苗都拔高了。然后他得意地对家里的人说："这几天真把我累坏了，我帮助稻苗长高了很多！"他儿子赶快 (hurriedly) 跑到地里一看，稻苗全都枯死了。

实用练习 Module Practice

你每星期一、三、五上午和星期二下午有必修课。现在你还需要选修五门选修课。请在下表中选出五门课，再写出一篇250字的文章，说明你为什么选修这五门课。

选修课课程表

	星期一	星期二	星期三	星期四	星期五
8:00–9:50AM	语法	语音	商务汉语	中国文学	中国音乐
10:10AM–12:00PM	中国文化	中国经济	汉字	写作	书法
2:00–3:50PM	书法	中国文学	武术	商务汉语	语法
4:00–5:30PM	写作	太极拳	语音	中国文化	中国电影
5:40–6:20PM	汉字	中国舞蹈	气功	中国经济	武术
6:30–7:50PM	中国音乐	中国电影	中国舞蹈	太极拳	气功

汉字笔顺 Stroke Order

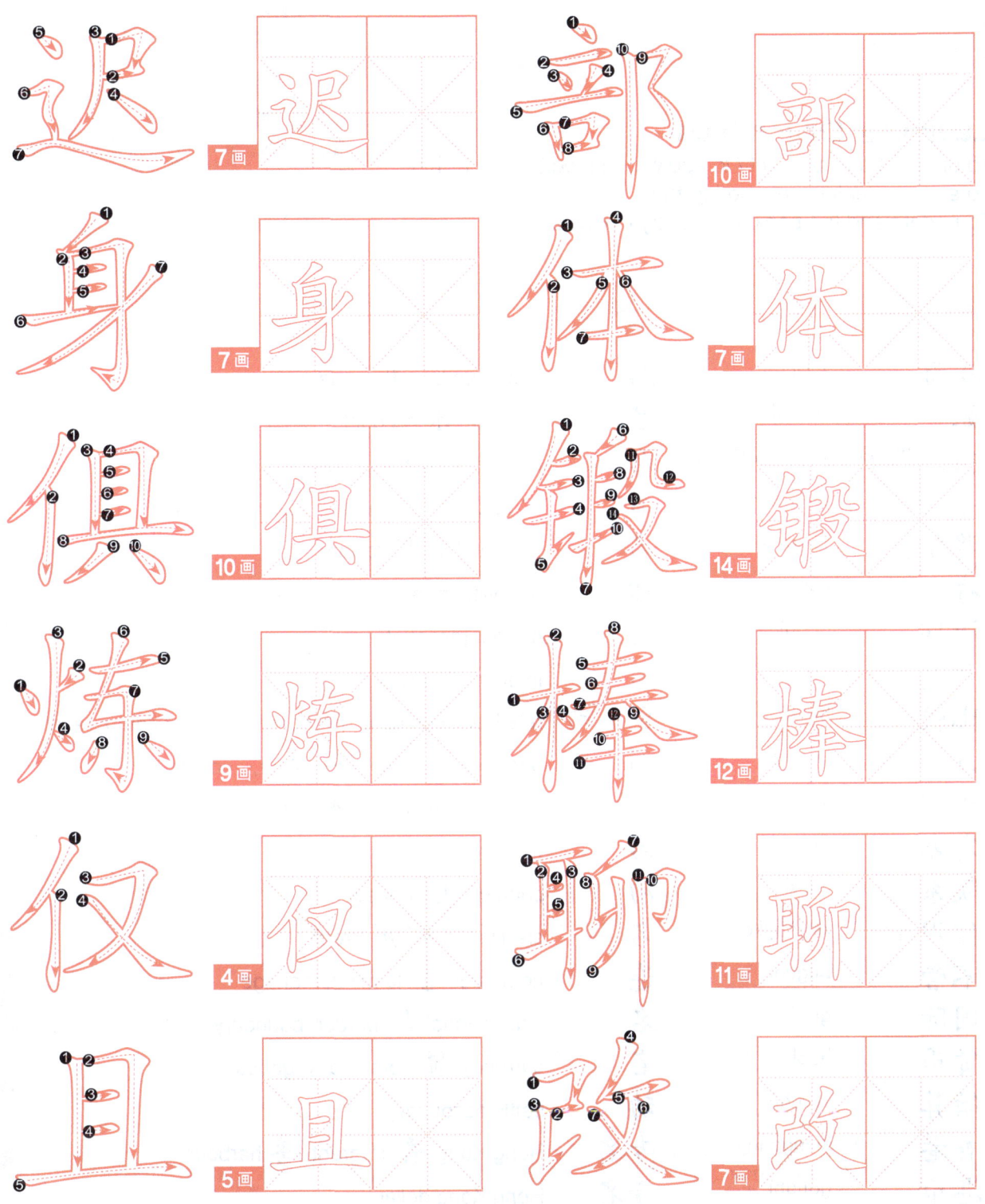

CHINESE IN STEPS 4   Lesson 33

33
第三十三课   在银行

Learning Objectives

To open a bank account / to apply for a credit card in China
To express feelings of good fortune
To understand the banking industry in China

生词 1 New Words

职员	zhíyuán	名	staff member 职 profession
账户	zhànghù	名	account 账 account
往来账户	wǎngláizhànghù	名	current account 往 toward
身份证	shēnfènzhèng	名	ID card 身份 identity, status 份 share
奖学金	jiǎngxuéjīn	名	scholarship 奖 reward
存	cún	动	deposit; store
活期	huóqī	名	current (account)
利息	lìxi	名	interest (financial)
比较	bǐjiào	副/动	relatively; compare 较 compared with; comparably
另外	lìngwài	副	besides, in addition 另 other, another
死期	sǐqī	名	fixed term (deposit account)
定期	dìngqī	名	fixed term
联系	liánxì	动	contact 联 connect
信用卡	xìnyòngkǎ	名	credit card 信用 credit
不管	bùguǎn	连	no matter 管 to mind; manage
国际	guójì	名	international 际 border, boundary
货币	huòbì	名	currency 货 commodity, goods
结算	jiésuàn	动	settle accounts
香港	Xiānggǎng	专名	Hong Kong 香 fragrant 港 harbour
港币	gǎngbì	专名	Hong Kong dollar

对话 1 Dialogue One

大卫：你好！我想开一个普通的往来账户。

职员：带身份证了没有？

大卫：我没有身份证。我带了护照。

职员：护照也可以。你有奖学金吗？

大卫：我不是学生，我在这儿工作。

职员：对不起。你在哪个公司工作？

大卫：可口可乐公司。

职员：你每月打算存多少钱？

大卫：两万块左右。

职员：活期账户利息比较低，你另外再开一个死期账户吧。

大卫：活期账户是往来账户，死期账户就是定期账户吧？

职员：对。

大卫：我先开一个活期账户，过几天再来开一个定期账户。

职员：好。请填一下这张表，把地址和联系电话写清楚。

大卫：另外，我想问一下，外国人可以申请信用卡吗？

职员：不管是外国人还是中国人，都可以在这里申请信用卡①。

大卫：我听说有个长城国际信用卡，以美元和港币结算③。

职员：对不起，该卡已经停办了。

大卫：那我申请一个长城人民币信用卡。

职员：好。请你再填一张表。请好好看一下说明再填。

🔊 生词2 New Words

丢	diū	动	lose
地址	dìzhǐ	名	address 址 site
单元	dānyuán	名	unit; module 单 single; bill 元 unit
密码	mìmǎ	名	pin number, password 密 secret
超市	chāoshì	名	supermarket
放心	fàngxīn	动	rest assured of
盗用	dàoyòng	动	embezzle 盗 steal
旧	jiù	形	old; used (not for age)
住处	zhùchù	名	dwelling 处 place; department
更改	gēnggǎi	动	change; alter
成为	chéngwéi	动	become
排行	páiháng	动/名	rank/ranking 排 put in order; row
名列	mingliè	动	list as 列 rank
多种多样	duōzhǒng duōyàng	形	various
系列	xìliè	名	series; serial
借记卡	jièjìkǎ	名	debit card
银联	Yínlián	名	UnionPay
美国运通	Měiguó yùntōng	专名	American Express
透支	tòuzhī	动	overdraft 透 permeate; transparent
使用	shǐyòng	动	utilise; use
标记	biāojì	名	mark 标 mark

🔊 补充词汇 Additional Vocabulary

账号	zhànghào	account number	自动取款机	zìdòngqǔkuǎnjī	ATM
结余	jiéyú	account balance	建设银行	Jiànshè Yínháng	China Construction Bank
贷款	dàikuǎn	loan	农业银行	Nóngyè Yínháng	Agricultural Bank of China
汇票	huìpiào	bill for remittance	交通银行	Jiāotōng Yínháng	Bank of Communications

维萨卡	wéisàkǎ	Visa (card)	工商银行	Gōngshāng Yínháng	Industrial and Commercial Bank of China
对账单	duìzhàngdān	bank statement	进出口银行	Jìnchūkǒu Yínháng	The Export-Import Bank of China

对话 2 Dialogue Two

职员：你好！这里是中国银行。

小方：你好。我的信用卡丢了。

职员：你的卡号是多少？

小方：00359486721。

职员：姓名？

小方：方英。

职员：电话？

小方：01359862417

职员：地址？

小方：香港路 25 号，9 号楼 2 单元 1 号。

职员：请说一下你的生日。

小方：1993 年 9 月 15 号。

职员：你的身份证号码后四位数字是多少？

小方：我记不清了，你等我一下，我找找身份证。啊，是"1225"。

职员：你最后一次使用信用卡是在什么时候，什么地方？

小方：今天中午，在超市里。我买了六十多块钱的东西。

职员：好，请放心，你的卡没有被盗用。

小方：谢天谢地②！

职员：你的旧卡已被停用，新卡很快就会寄到你的住处。你需要更改你的密码。

小方：我会换个新密码，非常感谢你的帮助。

职员：不客气。

 **课文 Text**

中国银行信用卡

中国银行是中国最重要的银行之一。2017年，中国银行在英国《银行家》杂志全球1000家大银行排行中，名列第4位。

中国银行的银行卡多种多样，其中长城卡系列深受人们的欢迎。长城借记卡系列包括长城人民币借记卡、长城校园卡和长城旅游借记卡等。长城信用卡系列包括长城人民币信用卡、长城银联熊猫卡和长城美国运通私人银行信用卡等。

在中国申请信用卡，除了你要有工作以外，你的账户里还要有现金。申请长城人民币信用卡普通卡时，你的账户里最少存有1000元人民币。你可以最高透支5000元。透支期，也就是信用期，为60天。你可以在标有中国银行长城信用卡标记的商店、饭店、酒楼、机场、医院等场所，使用长城信用卡结账。使用长城信用卡每年需交20元的年费。

语法注释 Grammar Notes

① 不管是外国人还是中国人，都可以在这里申请信用卡。
— "Everyone can apply for a credit card here, no matter whether they are Chinese or a foreigner."

不管……都…… is a construction with a sense of concession. 还是 is used to indicate alternative conditions.

> **For example:**
>
> (1) 不管是他来，他太太来，还是他女儿来，我们都十分欢迎。
> No matter whether he, his wife or his daughter comes, we'll still welcome them.
>
> (2) 不管他来还是不来，我们都应该准时 (on time) 开始。
> Regardless of whether he comes or not, we should still start on time.
>
> (3) 不管下不下雨，我都会在大门口等你。
> Whether it's raining or not, I'll still be waiting for you in the main entrance.

– 不管…… can also be used to indicate inclusiveness.

> **For example:**
>
> (4) 不管他怎么说，我们都应该准时开始。
> Regardless of what he says, we should still start on time.

② 谢天谢地！– expresses a strong sense of relief about something or that something is fortunate.

> **For example:**
>
> (1) 谢天谢地！你们都来了，我还以为你们都忘了呢。
> Thank heavens you've come, I thought you'd all forgotten.
>
> (2) 谢天谢地！我这次考试考得不错，九月可以去中国了。
> Thank goodness I've done quite well in these exams and can go to China in September.

③我听说有个长城国际信用卡，以美元和港币结算 – I heard that there is a Great Wall International Credit Card, which is settled in US dollars and Hong Kong dollars.

以……结算: to settle an account or a transaction in a nominated currency or a form of currency.

文化知识 Cultural Note

中国的银行业

The banking industry has been going through drastic changes since the introduction of the open door policy in China. With China's accession to the World Trade Organisation, the Chinese banking industry is being opened up to the world and foreign banks can deal in RMB business transactions now. All the major Chinese commercial banks have been restructured. As a result, business operations in most Chinese banks have become increasingly similar to those of foreign commercial banks. The Bank of China used to be the only bank dealing in foreign currencies, but nowadays all the major Chinese commercial banks provide services in both local and foreign currencies.

服务社会　创造价值

练习 Exercises

口语练习 Speaking Practice

角色扮演

1. A: 你刚到北京，去银行开一个新账户。
   B: 你是银行职员，你给A开账户。
2. A: 你的信用卡被偷了，你打电话去银行说明情况。
   B: 你是银行职员，你接听A的电话，为A的信用卡办理停用。

听力练习 Listening Practice

Listen to the following dialogues and choose the correct answer for each question.

1) a. 王府井　　　　　b. 天安门　　　　　c. 北京大学
2) a. 带现金　　　　　b. 电汇　　　　　　c. 带旅行支票
3) a. 找服务员　　　　b. 离开了　　　　　c. 一边看书一边排队
4) a. 他是外国人　　　b. 他要取外汇　　　c. 他要取人民币
5) a. 英镑　　　　　　b. 美元　　　　　　c. 人民币
6) a. 支行没有那么多钱　b. 他账户里没钱　　c. 他没带护照
7) a. 取钱表　　　　　b. 存钱表　　　　　c. 申请密码表
8) a. 银行关门了　　　b. 他忘了密码　　　c. 支行里没钱

语法练习 Grammar Practice

1. 多项选择

1) 我们可以用人民币 ____ 吗？
   a. 打算　　　　　　b. 都算　　　　　　c. 结算
2) ____ 信用卡都需要什么证件？
   a. 请求　　　　　　b. 申请　　　　　　c. 申要

3) 老王的行李箱打不开了，因为他把____忘了。
   a. 密码　　　　　　b. 密号　　　　　　c. 密数

4) ____是白猫还是黑猫，能抓住老鼠(lǎo shǔ)就是好猫。
   a. 不管　　　　　　b. 虽然　　　　　　c. 不仅

5) 不知道怎么搞的，我的电话号码被____了。
   a. 使用　　　　　　b. 盗用　　　　　　c. 偷盗

6) 我学汉语是想____一名翻译。
   a. 成为　　　　　　b. 是　　　　　　　c. 当成

7) 小李在汉语口语比赛中____第二。
   a. 当成　　　　　　b. 列名　　　　　　c. 名列

8) 我想开一个人民币账户，____再开一个美元账户。
   a. 而且　　　　　　b. 另外　　　　　　c. 不过

2. 选词填空

了、多少、过、最高的、先进、站着、进口、当时

　　昨天上午我和我的同学到____上海。下午，我们就到南京路去买东西。十年前，我和我的父母亲来____上海，我记得上海是一座漂亮的古城(gǔ)(ancient city)，当时，并没有____高楼。黄河路上的国际饭店只有24层，可是____已经算是有名的高楼了。十年后的今天，上海到处都是高楼。____有88层。当年的国际饭店还在那里____，可是成了一个小弟弟。上海现在也有了地铁。上海的地铁比伦敦的还漂亮、还____。上海商店里的东西真多，有中国制造的，也有外国____的。人们高高兴兴地选择他们心爱的商品。

认字识词 Words with Known Characters

1. 查找出下列词语的词义，并翻译成英文。

管理 _____	管家 _____
账本 _____	算账 _____
奖金 _____	丢面子 _____
提货单 _____	寄存处 _____
香水 _____	香米 _____

2. 翻译下列词语，并找出其结构规律。请至少再找出五个同样结构的词。

道路 _____	喜爱 _____
数量 _____	变化 _____
歌唱 _____	城市 _____
光亮 _____	生产 _____
表格 _____	等候 _____
偷盗 _____	存放 _____

翻译练习 Translation

Say the following sentences in Chinese first and then write them out in characters.

1) No matter whether he goes or not, we shall go tomorrow anyway.
2) Thank goodness my wallet didn't go missing. I nearly stopped my credit card.
3) Credit cards nowadays all require a pin number.
4) If you want to apply for this job, you need to fill in the form and send it to that company.
5) There are a lot of people in Hong Kong. Buildings there are usually tall, but roomsare comparatively small.
6) It is really convenient to go to the cash machine to withdraw money. You can withdraw whenever you want.

阅读 Reading

成语故事 The stories behind Chinese idioms

画蛇添足 (huàshétiānzú)

楚国有个贵族(aristocrat)赏(shǎng)(bestowed)给他手下的人一壶(hú)(pot)酒。如果大家一起喝，这壶酒是不够(gòu)(enough)的。于是，大家商量了一下，决定每个人在地上画一条蛇，谁先画好就把这壶酒给谁喝。

有个人画得很快，不一会儿就画好了。他拿起酒壶刚要喝，回头一看，别人都还没有画好，便给蛇添(tiān)(add)起脚来。正在这时候，另外一个人画好了。那人马上夺过酒壶说："蛇本来没有脚，你为什么要给它画脚呢？这壶酒该我喝。"说完，他咕嘟咕嘟(gū dū)(glug)把酒喝光了。

实用练习 Module Practice

银行网页

以下是一家中国银行的网址主页。你的朋友想了解怎样开一个活期的人民币账户，他/她应该查看哪个/些标题？如果他/她想要开信用卡呢？

银行风貌	个人金融	银行卡	金融咨询	网上论坛	商城	理财	保险
人才招聘	企业金融	机构业务	投资银行	资产托管	基金	外汇	股票
资产处置	电子银行	网上银行	电话银行	手机银行	黄金	债券	北京

汉字笔顺 Stroke Order

CHINESE IN STEPS 4 Lesson 33

34

第三十四课　寄包裹

Learning Objectives
To send a parcel via delivery service or in a post office
To specify essential conditions
To understand the Chinese lunar calendar

生词 1 New Words

包裹	bāoguǒ	名	parcel 裹 wrap
邮局	yóujú	名	post office 邮 post 局 bureau
快递	kuàidì	名	express delivery 递 hand over
准时	zhǔnshí	形	on time
保险	bǎoxiǎn	形	safe
顺丰	Shùnfēng	专名	SF Express 顺 along
申通	Shēntōng	专名	STO Express Co
中国邮政	Zhōngguó yóuzhèng	专名	China Post 政 certain administrative aspects of government
外资	wàizī	名	foreign investment 资 capital
绣花	xiùhuā	动+名	embroidery 绣 embroider
睡衣	shuìyī	名	pyjamas
被套	bèitào	名	quilt cover 被 quilt 套 cover;（量）a set of
床单	chuángdān	名	bed sheet 单 sheet
手工	shǒugōng	名	handmade; handwork
奶奶	nǎinai	名	grandma
从事	cóngshì	动	engaged in (for a job)
业务	yèwù	名	business, professional work

四十七　47

对话 1 Dialogue One

李健：张红，我想寄一个包裹，学校附近有没有邮局？

张红：现在大家都不去邮局寄东西了，都找快递公司！

李健：快递公司的服务怎么样？能像邮局那样准时和保险吗？

张红：当然能。快递公司还可以上门取货①。

李健：那可就方便多了。中国都有什么快递公司？

张红：比较大的有顺丰和申通。

李健：有没有外资快递公司？比如 EMS 或者⑤ DHL？

张红：有。你要寄什么东西？

李健：一件绣花睡衣、一个绣花被套，还有一条床单。

张红：看来你很喜欢中国的手工绣花制品。

李健：不是我，是我奶奶喜欢。她一定要我买些寄回去。

张红：你寄到哪儿？

李健：马德里。我奶奶住在马德里。

张红：那你选择中国邮政吧。他们和 EMS 合作，主要从事国际快递业务③。

李健：谢谢。

🔊 生词 2 New Words

纪念	jìniàn	名/动	commemorate 念 miss; read, study
邮票	yóupiào	名	stamp
属	shǔ	动	be born in the year of, belong to
属相	shǔxiàng	名	signs of the Chinese zodiac
阴历	yīnlì	名	Chinese lunar calendar
阳历	yánglì	名	solar calendar; Gregorian calendar 阳 sun; masculine
历法	lìfǎ	名	calendar
相差	xiāngchà	动	differ from each other 相 each other
月份	yuèfèn	名	month
当年	dāngnián	名	at that time (year)
比如	bǐrú	动	for example
原来	yuánlái	副	in fact, actually, originally 原 original
由	yóu	介	by
万国邮联	Wànguó yóulián	专名	Universal Postal Union (UPU) 万 ten thousand
管理	guǎnlǐ	动/名	manage; management
到达	dàodá	动/名	arrive; arrivals 达 reach
轮船	lúnchuán	名	steamship 轮 wheel
运输	yùnshū	名/动	transport 输 transport; lose
海运	hǎiyùn	名	transport by sea, surface mail 运 transport
空运	kōngyùn	名	transport by air, airmail 空 sky; air
或者	huòzhě	连	or 或 or
到底	dàodǐ	副	ultimately, in the end, after all
价格	jiàgé	名	price 价 value, price
大型	dàxíng	形	large size 型 type
紧急	jǐnjí	形	urgent, emergency 紧 tight 急 pressing

补充词汇 Additional Vocabulary

鼠	shǔ	mouse	鸟	niǎo	bird
虎	hǔ	tiger	鹅	é	goose
兔	tù	rabbit	驴	lú	donkey
蛇	shé	snake	狼	láng	wolf
羊	yáng	sheep/goat	狐狸	húli	fox
猴	hóu	monkey	狮子	shīzi	lion

对话 2 Dialogue Two

王：小李，猪年的纪念邮票出来了，你看，漂亮吧？！

李：真漂亮！

王：你不是也属猪吗？快去邮局买 几套② 吧。

李：我不属猪，我属狗。

王：怎么会呢？！我们都是1994年出生的。

李：可我的生日是在阳历1月，那时阴历还是1993年12月呢。

王：阴历和阳历⑥ 到底是怎么回事？我不太懂。

李：阳历是西方人使用的历法，阴历是中国人使用的历法。

王：为什么会有两种不同的历法呢？

李：因为西方人是以太阳来计算的，而中国人是以月亮来计算的。

王：我明白了。那阴历和阳历相差几天？

李：一个多月。

王：所以一月份出生的人不一定属当年的属相。

李：不仅仅是一月份，二月初出生的人也不一定。比如说小方。

王：怪不得小方的床头上挂着一只小狗，原来他也是属狗的。

课文 Text

从中国寄包裹到英国

EMS（Express Mail Service）中文名为邮政特快专递服务，是目前中国使用最多的国际快递公司。EMS 由万国邮联管理④，在中国属于中国邮政快递服务。EMS 有三种运输方式：航空包裹、空运水陆路包裹、水陆路包裹。简单地说就是空运、空运加海运和陆运、海运和陆运。

航空包裹最快，从北京到伦敦最快三天就可以到达，但邮费比较贵。空运水陆路包裹是使用国际航班、汽车、火车或者轮船来运输的，时间上比航空包裹慢，通常需要十天左右，但邮费比较便宜。水陆路包裹是不通过航空运输，只使用汽车、火车或者轮船来运输的一种方式，因此这是最慢的一种。从中国到英国，最快需要一个月，最慢需要三个月。水陆路包裹价格是最便宜的。

到底哪一种方式比较好呢？航空邮件适合比较紧急的快件；水陆路适合大型的、不紧急的包裹；空运水陆路适合所有的包裹。

语法注释 Grammar Notes

① 上门取货 – pick up at home.

② 几套 – 几 means several here when used in a statement, and refers to an indefinite number usually under ten. It goes before a measure word.

For example:

(1) 北京的秋天天气很好，我想在北京多住几天。
The weather in Beijing is very good in autumn. I'm thinking of staying for a few more days.

(2) 那天晚上很冷，酒吧里只有几个人。
It was very cold that evening and there were only a few people in the bar.

③ 主要从事国际快递业务 – Mainly engaged in international express delivery business 从事 – be engaged in

For example:

(1) 王先生一直从事进出口业务。
Mr. Wang has been engaged in the import and export business.

(2) 她不想从事全职工作。
She does not want to work full time.

④ EMS 由万国邮联管理 – EMS is managed by the UPU.
由……管理 – managed by

For example:

(1) 老董事长走了，这家公司由新人管理。
The old chairman has left; this company is managed by a new person.

(2) 学校的酒吧是由学生会来管理的。
The college's bar is managed by the student union.

⑤ 或者 – means "or" in a statement, while 还是 is used in a question.

For example:

(1) 明天或者你来、或者我去，怎么都行。
Tomorrow either you come here or I'll go there, either way is fine.

(2) 您要买长裙还是短裙？
Do you want to buy a long skirt or a short one?

⑥ 阴历 and 阳历 – There are 3 different calendar in the world: the Gregorian Calendar (阳历), which is based on the Sun; the lunar calendar (阴历), which is based on the Moon; and the traditional Chinese calendar (农历 nónglì – agricultural calendar), which is calculated with regards to the movement of both the Moon and the Sun and is thus mistakenly called 阴历. Both 阳历 and 阴

历 are used in China now. 阳历 is used for most day-to-day activities, but all traditional Chinese holidays – as well as auspicious dates for events such as weddings or the opening of a business – are calculated according to the lunar calendar. Traditionally, the name of each year repeats itself in a cycle of 60 years as it consists of a combination of two orderly characters, one from the 10 Heavenly Stems (天干) and the other from the 12 Earthly Branches (地支).

文化知识 Cultural Note

中国人的属相

There are twelve animals in the Chinese zodiac, and each corresponds to one of the Earthly Branches. These Earthly Branches relate to the Chinese lunar calendar, and they form part of the Chinese system for naming years. These animal signs follow a strict 12-year cycle as listed below. Since they are calculated according to the lunar calendar the starting point of each animal year is the first day of the Chinese New Year. The Chinese new year period is also known as Spring Festival. So, if 2000 was the Year of Dragon, can you work out which animal year you were born in?

The 12 animals are: rat, ox, tiger, hare, dragon, snake, horse, sheep, monkey, rooster, dog, pig.

CHINESE IN STEPS 4   Lesson 34

练习 Exercises

口语练习 Speaking Practice

角色扮演

a. 你想寄个生日礼物，但不知道怎么寄，也不知道用哪种方式邮寄好。

b. 你是邮局职员，你告诉A怎么寄，用哪种方式寄最好。

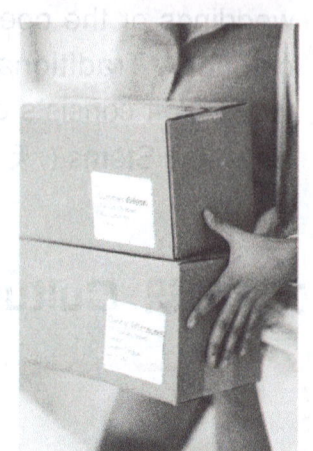

听力练习 Listening Practice

Listen to the following dialogues and choose the correct answer for each question.

1)	a. 领带	b. 睡衣	c. 明信片
2)	a. 我们欢迎你	b. 北京欢迎你	c. 中国欢迎你
3)	a. 她妹妹要两套	b. 她要两套	c. 她和妹妹一人一套
4)	a. 旗袍	b. 绣花睡衣	c. 床单
5)	a. 绣花睡衣	b. 明信片	c. 中国画儿
6)	a. 包	b. 信封	c. 箱子
7)	a. 水	b. 药	c. 酒
8)	a. 背疼	b. 腿疼	c. 牙疼
9)	a. 不能空运	b. 便宜	c. 快
10)	a. 750	b. 650	c. 550

语法练习 Grammar Practice

1. 多项选择

1) 我不喜欢 _____ 房地产业务。

　　a. 从事　　　　　　b. 从来　　　　　　c. 理事

2) 张先生有一套熊猫____邮票。
   a. 记录　　　　　b. 几年　　　　　c. 纪念

3) 星期天大家都喜欢出去玩儿，马路上____都是人。
   a. 到处　　　　　b. 到来　　　　　c. 走来

4) 我十二点前____要赶到火车站，十二点以后就没有车了。
   a. 一起　　　　　b. 一共　　　　　c. 一定

5) 在我们这儿，有些东西是不能邮寄的，____狗和猫。
   a. 不比　　　　　b. 比如　　　　　c. 如果

6) 真没想到_____你我是校友。
   a. 原来　　　　　b. 本来　　　　　c. 和

7) 属龙的和属猪的_____几岁？
   a. 不到　　　　　b. 相差　　　　　c. 差不多

8) 李英_____是美国人还是加拿大人？
   a. 到底　　　　　b. 到来　　　　　c. 要是

2. 选词填空

使用、到、一般、中间、只有、小月、如、又

历法____分为三类：太阴历、太阳历和阴阳历，太阴历和太阳历____简称为阴历、阳历。中国____的农历，一般人把它叫做阴历，这是不对的。农历是阴阳历。农历每一个月初一都正好是月亮在太阳和地球____，农历的一个月是从新月出现的那一天____下一个新月出现的前一天。农历的大月是三十天，____是二十九天。但是农历和阳历不同，大小月不固定。____春节的前一天常称为大年三十，但有时候，如2000的农历十二月就____二十九天。

CHINESE IN STEPS 4   Lesson 34

认字识词 Words with Known Characters

1. 查找出下列词语的词义，并翻译成英文。

邮递员	_____	顺利	_____
念书	_____	车轮	_____
太阳	_____	办事处	_____
阳光	_____	月光	_____
邮电局	_____	警察局	_____

2. 翻译下列词语，并找出其结构规律。请至少再找出五个同样结构的词。

始终	_____	长短	_____
阴阳	_____	是非	_____
老少	_____	冷热	_____
真假	_____	死活	_____
来往	_____	文武	_____
早晚	_____	轻重	_____

翻译练习 Translation

Say the following sentences in Chinese first and then write them out in characters.

1) This post office is managed by China Post.
2) I would like to buy some souvenir stamps of Beijing.
3) I was born in 1985. Do you know which Chinese zodiac animal I am?
4) I used to eat meat, but my doctor told me that I'd better eat more vegetables and fruit. I haven't eaten meat since.
5) Why is the parcel I sent from China last month not here yet?
6) How did you post your parcel? By air or by sea?

阅读 Reading

成语故事 The stories behind Chinese idioms

守株待兔

宋(sòng)国有个农夫。有一天,他正在田里干活。突然,从远处跑来一只兔子,一下子撞(zhuàng)(bump)在稻(dào)田(tián)(paddy field)旁边的大树上,当场就倒地死了。农夫看到之后,赶快跑过去把死兔子捡(jiǎn)(pick)起来,开心地带回家吃了。从此以后,这个农夫天天坐在大树旁,等着兔子再来撞树。他等啊等,可是他不仅没有捡到兔子,连兔子的影子也没见着!农夫的那几块地,却因为太久没有耕种(gēngzhòng)(cultivated),都荒芜(huāng wú)(weed-filled)了。

实用练习 Module Practice

你在邮局寄包裹，试填下列两张表格。

国内普通包裹详情单

收件人	□□□□□□		接收局编号：
	详细地址：	内装何物及数量	
	姓名：		
	电话：		收寄人名章
寄件人	详细地址：	是否保价	重量：　　　　克
			单价：　　　元/千克
		是（　） 否（　）	挂号费：　　　　元
	姓名：	保价金额：	保价费：　　　　元
	电话：	备注	回执费：　　　　元
	邮编：		总计：　　　　元

国内快递包裹详情单

收件人	□□□□□□		接收局编号：
	详细地址：	内装何物及数量	
	姓名：		
	电话：		收寄人名章
寄件人	详细地址：	是否保价	重量：　　　　克
			单价：　　　元/千克
		是（　） 否（　）	挂号费：　　　　元
	姓名：	保价金额：	保价费：　　　　元
	电话：	备注	回执费：　　　　元
	邮编：		总计：　　　　元

汉字笔顺 Stroke Order

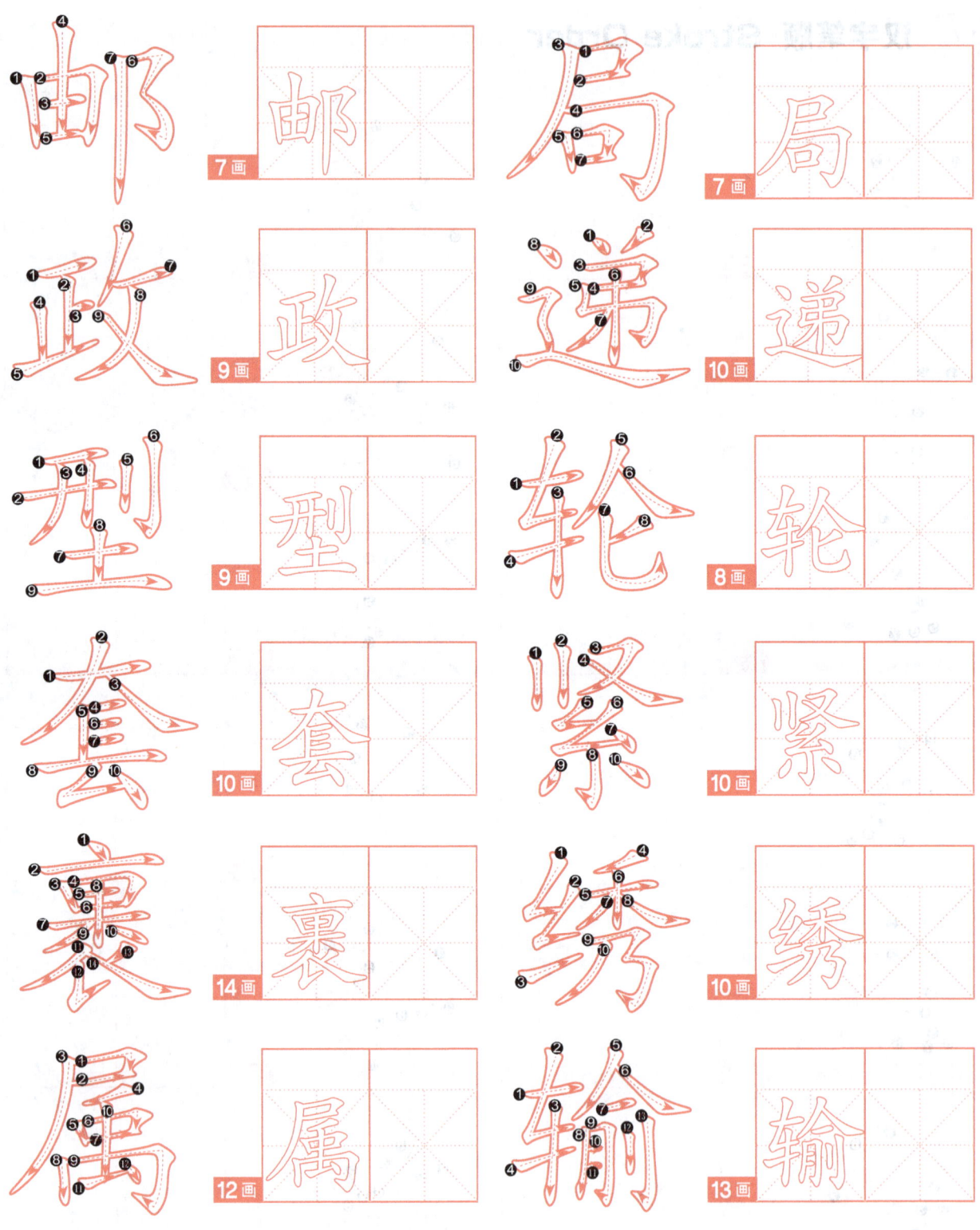

35
第三十五课　理发

Learning Objectives
To get your hair styled and comment on appearance
To use the verbal construction V + 起来
To learn about the modifier + keyword construction

🔊 生词 1 New Words

发型	fàxíng	名	hair style 发 hair 型 style; model
理发店	lǐfàdiàn	名	hairdressing salon 理发 hair cut
市中心	shìzhōngxīn	名	city centre
剪	jiǎn	动	cut
吹	chuī	动	blow dry
连剪带吹	liánjiǎndàichuī		cut and blow (hair)
女士	nǚshì	名	lady, madam 士 person
美发	měifà	动 + 名	have one's hair styled
烫发	tàngfà	动 + 名	perm one's hair 烫 scald, burn
染发	rǎnfà	动 + 名	colour or dye hair 染 (to) colour
东单	Dōngdān	专名	a shopping street in Beijing
预约	yùyuē	动 / 名	reserve; reservation

🔊 补充词汇 Additional Vocabulary

洗发液/水	xǐfàyè/shuǐ	shampoo	卷发器	juǎnfàqì	curler
护发素	hùfàsù	conditioner	吹风机	chuīfēngjī	hair dryer
发乳	fàrǔ	hair cream	电动推子	diàndòngtuīzi	hair clippers
发胶	fàjiāo	hair spray	剪子	jiǎnzi	scissors
冷烫液	lěngtàngyè	perm lotion	梳子	shūzi	comb

对话 1 Dialogue One

小方：小王，你去哪儿了？我到处找你。

小王：我去邮局了。找我有事吗？

小方：你的发型不错，我想问问你是在哪家理发店理的。

小王：我是在市中心的一家理发店理的。

小方：那家店叫什么名字？

小王：新新美发。

小方：贵不贵？

小王：不贵。连剪带吹①一共才五十五块。

小方：那里有没有女士美发部？

小王：有，那里不仅理发，而且还烫发和染发。

小方：太好了！我女朋友要染发，我们可以一起去了。理发店几⑤点开门？

小王：八点。这家理发店很忙，你需要预约。

小方：知道了。你有这家理发店的地址吗？

小王：没有，理发店就在东单，你上网查一下就知道了。

小方：好的，谢谢。

小王：不客气。

🔊 生词 2 New Words

排队	páiduì	动	queue
轮	lún	动/名	become one's turns; turn, wheel
显眼	xiǎnyǎn	形	conspicuous 显 reveal, show
引起	yǐnqǐ	动	cause, give rise to 引 guide
注意	zhùyì	动/名	pay attention; attention, notice
短	duǎn	形	short
平头	píngtóu	名	cropped hair 平 even, level
帅	shuài	形	smart; handsome
精神	jīngshén	形/名	smart looking; lively 精 smart 神 spirit; god
脸型	liǎnxíng	名	feature (of the face)
开业	kāiyè	动	start/open (a business)
老字号	lǎozìhào	名	long established brand (shop)
美容	měiróng	动+名	cosmetology; improve one's looks
美容师	měiróng shī	名	beautician
位于	wèiyú	动	situated at/in 于 at, in; a surname
王府井	Wángfǔjǐng	专名	a shopping street in Beijing 府 mansion 井 well
大街	dàjiē	名	broadway; avenue 街 street
西单	Xīdān	专名	a shopping street in Beijing
之一	zhīyī		one of 之 of; object substitute
出色	chūsè	形	outstanding
理发师	lǐfàshī	名	barber
设计	shèjì	动	design
改造	gǎizào	动	transform
顾客	gùkè	名	customer 顾 look after
不同	bùtóng	形	different 同 same, similar
提供	tígōng	动	provide 供 supply
贵宾	guìbīn	名	VIP 宾 guest
相应	xiāngyìng	形	corresponding
四联美发厅	Sìlián měifàtīng	专名	Silian Hairdressing

美白美发厅　Měibái měifàtīng　专名　Meibai Hairdressing

对话2 Dialogue Two

理发员：你们好！请进。

小　方：谢谢。啊，这么多人排队！

理发员：你们预约了没有？

小　方：我们在网上预约了，两点。

理发员：好，你先坐一会儿。一会儿就轮到你了。请坐。

小　方：谢谢。

理发员：这位女士是来美发的吧？

小　李：对，我想把头发染成黑色的。

理发员：你的金发很漂亮，染成黑色太可惜了。

小　李：我的金发在这儿太显眼了。我不想引起人们的注意。

小　方：师傅，我想理一个短发，平头。

理发员：好。你理平头一定很帅②。

小　李：我早就想让他换个发型，短发看起来③很精神。

小　方：洗起来③也方便。

理发员：没错儿④。又精神又方便，而且很适合你的脸型。

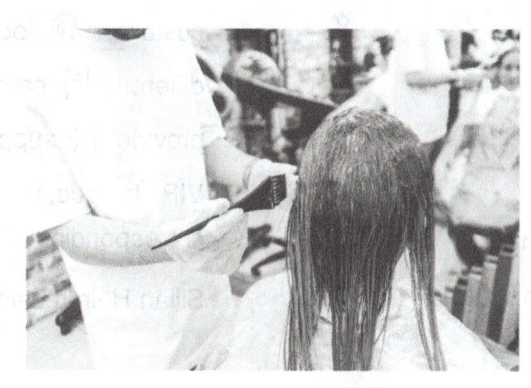

课文 Text

北京四联美发厅

北京市很大，有几百个理发店，有名的理发店也有几十⑤个。王府井大街的"四联美发厅"就是有名的理发店之一。"四联美发厅"是由"四联美发厅"与"美白美发厅"合并而成的。"美白美发厅"于1928年开业，是北京的一家老字号，当时叫"美白理发馆"。五十年代，为了支援北京的服务行业，上海的四家理发名店组成"四联理发馆"，于1956年搬到北京。九十年代，"四联美发厅"与"美白美发厅"合并。

"四联美发厅"有很多出色的理发师和美容师。搬到王府井大街后，"四联美发厅"重新进行了设计改造。一楼为"女宾理发"，二楼为"男宾理发"、三楼为"美容室"。同时，"四联美发厅"还设立了男宾美发的"贵宾厅"和女宾美发的"名人室"，为不同的顾客提供相应的服务。

语法注释 Grammar Notes

① 连剪带吹 – 连……带…… is a set construction linking two items.

For example:

(1) 那家饭店不贵，昨天我们五个人连吃带喝才花了一百英镑。
That restaurant is not dear. Yesterday it came to less than £100 for five of us including both food and drinks.

(2) 他们玩得很高兴，连喝带唱一直玩到晚上十二点才休息。
They had a good time drinking and singing till twelve o'clock at night before they went to bed.

② 你理平头一定很帅 – If you had your hair cut short, you would definitely look smart. In Chinese, the conjunction 如果 can often be omitted. The full sentence is 如果你理平头，你(看上去)一定很帅。

③ 看起来 and 洗起来 – 起来 as a complement has the sense of "start to", "when one comes to". 看起来 is a set phrase, meaning "look" or "seem". In 洗起来, 起来 has the sense of "when you come to wash it".

For example:

(1) 说起来容易，做起来就难了。
It's easy to say but hard to do.

(2) 这菜看起来不怎么样，可吃起来很不错。
This dish doesn't look much, but it's delicious when you come to eat it.

④ 没错儿 – a colloquial expression of agreement that is particularly popular in Beijing and means "right", "absolutely".

⑤ "几"，"十几" 和 "几十" 的用法 – 几 is used as an unspecified number between 1 and 9 to indicate an imprecise amount, like "several" in English. Hence, 十几 refers to a number between eleven and nineteen, similar to "a dozen or so" in English, while 几十 means somewhere between ten and one hundred, similar to "dozens" in English. Note that while you can say 十几 or 几十, you can only say 几百 "hundreds" or 几千 "thousands", not the other way round. Remember to use measure word as these are numbers.

For example:

(1) 我这学期只有几门课。
I only have a few classes this semester.

(2) 我们昨天花了十几块钱打的去学校上课。
Yesterday we spent over ten yuan taking a taxi to college to attend class.

(3) 大门口站着几十个人，男的女的都有。
There are several dozen people, both male and female, standing at the main entrance.

文化知识 Cultural Note

中国的美容卫生服务业

Services involving beauty and hygiene in China have changed dramatically over the last few decades, especially in urban areas and cosmopolitan cities. Most of these services, excluding beauty treatment, were in existence before, but the nature and scope of the services were limited. The care in public bathhouses was mostly restricted to hair and feet (including pedicure). New beauty services have emerged as a result of much improved standards of living as well as changed lifestyles among younger generations. Today it is not uncommon to see young women having beauty treatment in beauty salons (which usually also do hair). International beauty salons open their chain stores in China, so you can even find a Mohican-style haircut on the Chinese high street.

CHINESE IN STEPS 4   Lesson 35

练习 Exercises

口语练习 Speaking Practice

角色扮演

a. 你去理发店或美发厅理发或美发。你告诉理发师上次做得不好，你希望这次理发师能按照你的想法做。

b. 你是理发师，你会想方设法让顾客满意。

听力练习 Listening Practice

Listen to the following dialogues and choose the correct answer for each question.

1) a. 她穿新衣服了　　b. 她换发型了　　　　c. 她瘦了
2) a. 她不喜欢小王　　b. 她的头发太长了　　c. 她的头发太短了
3) a. 想变漂亮　　　　b. 剪短发便宜　　　　c. 短发方便
4) a. 理发师的错　　　b. 小李的错　　　　　c. 明星的错
5) a. 黑色　　　　　　b. 黄色　　　　　　　c. 红色
6) a. 小李　　　　　　b. 理发师们都说　　　c. 那个理发师
7) a. 经理不在　　　　b. 给她剪头的就是经理　c. 不想找经理
8) a. 她男朋友的妹妹　b. 她妹妹　　　　　　c. 经理的妹妹

语法练习 Grammar Practice

1. 多项选择

1) 我家在伦敦的南_____，三区。
   a. 边　　　　　　b. 部　　　　　　　c. 方

2) 短发看起来很_____。
   a. 精神　　　　　b. 精力　　　　　　c. 精美

3) 他的发型_____了大家的注意。

    a. 形成　　　　　b. 引起　　　　　c. 引出

4) 我没有 _____ 他是什么时候走的。
    a. 意思　　　　　b. 注视　　　　　c. 注意

5) 大家都穿校服，你一个人穿便服，你不觉得太 _____ 了吗？
    a. 精神　　　　　b. 帅　　　　　　c. 显眼

6) 你对教学工作还很不熟悉，应该好好提高一下 ____ 水平。
    a. 服务　　　　　b. 业务　　　　　c. 家务

7) 老钱的太太在 ____ 店工作。
    a. 理发　　　　　b. 剪发　　　　　c. 发型

8) ____ 们先生们，谢谢你们来参加今天的晚会。
    a. 女人　　　　　b. 女子　　　　　c. 女士

2. 选词填空

以外、只能、起来、虽然、而是、可以、
只好、顾客、让、还是

路易斯（Louis）走进了车站理发馆，他想 ____ 车站的理发师给他理个发。他家就在车站附近，这里除了车站理发馆 ____，再没有别的理发馆了。路易斯对理发师说："现在店里没有 _____，能不能给我理理发？"理发师说："非常抱歉，按照规定（ànzhào guīdìng）（according to rules），我 _____ 为手里有车票的顾客服务。"路易斯没办法，____ 买了一张火车票。可是理发师 ____ 不给他理发。理发师说："我们这儿是为坐火车的顾客服务的。_____ 你买了车票，可是你没有坐车啊！"路易斯非常生气，大叫 _____。这时候理发师拿起了电话，打完电话后他对路易斯说："好了，你 _____ 理发了。"路易斯高兴极了，可是理发师说："不是在这儿，____ 在下一站。下一站的理发师正在等着给你理发呢。"

CHINESE IN STEPS 4　　*Lesson 35*

认字识词 Words with Known Characters

1. 查找出下列词语的词义，并翻译成英文。

护士	_____	平常	_____
明显	_____	总之	_____
洗钱	_____	洗礼	_____
照顾	_____	宾馆	_____
染色体	_____	井井有条	_____

2. 翻译下列词语，并找出其结构规律。请至少再找出五个同样结构的词。

黑豆	_____	明文	_____
红牌	_____	黄牌	_____
美酒	_____	香菜	_____
怪话	_____	短路	_____
平地	_____	冷盘	_____
空位	_____	旧车	_____

翻译练习 Translation

Say the following sentences in Chinese first and then write them out in characters.

1) I like short hair, as it is very easy to wash.
2) Hair colouring and curling are very cheap there. It would not cost more than 80 pounds altogether.
3) He seems a bit angry. I know that he hasn't had a break for over a month now.
4) London is situated in the south-east of the UK. It is not very far from the sea.
5) Mr Wang is an outstanding barber; he cuts hair extremely well.
6) There are many people in the queue; it will take a couple of hours before it is your turn.

阅读 Reading

成语故事 The stories behind Chinese idioms

掩耳盗铃 (yǎn ěr dào líng)

春秋战国时期有一个小偷，他看中了一口钟，想把它偷走。可是钟太笨重了，他很难搬走。他就找来了一把锤(chuí)子，想把钟敲碎(qiāo suì)(break up)了再搬走。可是他一敲下去，钟就发出了巨大(jù dà)(very big)的响声。他怕人们听到响声来抓(zhuā)(seize)他，就把自己的耳朵捂(wǔ)(cover)上了再敲。他想："既然我离得这么近都听不见，其他人当然更听不见了。"当然别人还是听到了钟声，小偷被抓住了。

实用练习 Module Practice

下面是一个美发店的服务价目表。请写一封电子邮件预定理发或美发时间。你要写明你是谁；你要什么样的服务；要什么时候去和你的联系电话等等。你还可以问问收不收信用卡；美发店附近有没有地铁站、可以不可以停车等等。

天天理发店价目表

男士剪发		女士美发美容	
理光头	25元	剪短发	30元
理长发	35元	剪长发	40元
理平头	55元	洗头	15元
洗头	10元	吹风	15元
吹风	10元	染发	45元
染发	35元	烫发	50元

营业时间：上午八点——晚上九点。为避免(bì miǎn)(avoid)长时间排队等待，请打电话或发电子邮件预约 Ttmf@163.com

汉字笔顺 Stroke Order

36
第三十六课 请假

Learning Objectives
To ask someone to pass on a sick-leave message
To write a short note asking for leave
To learn about the verb-object construction

🔊 生词 1 New Words

羊肉串	yángròu chuàn	名	lamb skewer 羊 goat, sheep 串 bunch
拉肚子	lādùzi	动	have diarrhoea 拉 pull; defecate
新鲜	xīnxiān	形	fresh
熟	shóu	形	cooked; ripe
请假	qǐngjià	动	ask for leave
请假条	qǐngjiàtiáo	名	written request for leave/absence 条 note, slip of paper
替	tì	动/介	substitute; on behalf of
哎	āi	感叹	ah
现成	xiànchéng	形	ready-made, off the shelf
例子	lìzi	名	example 例 instance
抄	chāo	动	copy
签	qiān	动	sign
自己	zìjǐ	代	oneself 己 oneself
原因	yuányīn	名	cause, reason
相同	xiāngtóng	形	the same
笨	bèn	形	stupid, slow
方法	fāngfǎ	名	method
聪明	cōngming	形	intelligent, clever 聪 clever

🗣️ 🔊 对话 1 Dialogue One

小王：小李，快起床，上课要迟到了！

小李：我今天不舒服，不能去上课了。

小王：你怎么啦？哪儿不舒服？

小李：我昨晚吃了些羊肉串，<u>没想到</u>①拉起肚子来了。

小王：是不是羊肉不新鲜？

小李：<u>谁知道呢</u>②！也可能是没有烤熟。

小王：要不要去医院看看？

小李：不用了，我已经吃药了。

小王：那你好好休息，我帮你请假。

小李：我给老师写个请假条吧。

小王：你能写吗？<u>要不要我替你写</u>③？

小李：不用，我自己能写。哎，你知道怎么用中文写请假条吗？

小王：书上有现成的例子，抄一个签上自己的名字就行了。

小李：那怎么行！请假的原因不可能相同啊！

小王：你真笨，你把头疼改成拉肚子就行了。

小李：这是个好方法！还是你聪明。

🔊 补充词汇 Additional Vocabulary

嗓子疼	sǎngziténg	sore throat	肺炎	fèiyán	pneumonia
腿疼	tuǐténg	leg pains	胃炎	wèiyán	gastritis
腰疼	yāoténg	back pain	皮炎	píyán	dermatitis
骨折	gǔzhé	fracture (bone)	过敏	guòmǐn	allergy; allergic
腿断了	tuǐduànle	broken leg	心脏病	xīnzàngbìng	heart disease
脚崴了	jiǎowǎile	sprained ankle	高血压	gāoxuèyā	high blood pressure

CHINESE IN STEPS 4   Lesson 36

🔊 生词 2 New Words

好像	hǎoxiàng	副	seem, like
通知	tōngzhī	名/动	notice; notify
关于	guānyú	介	about, regarding
讲座	jiǎngzuò	名	lecture 讲 talk
通告	tōnggào	名	public notice, announcement
更加	gèngjiā	副	even more
正式	zhèngshì	形	formal
范围	fànwéi	名	scope, range 范 limits 围 all round
对内	duìnèi	介宾结构	internal 内 inner
对外	duìwài	介宾结构	external
内部	nèibù	名	internal; interior
公开	gōngkāi	动	publicize
广告	guǎnggào	名	advertisement 告 tell
区别	qūbié	名/动	difference 区 area, zone
商业	shāngyè	名	commerce; business
告诉	gàosù	动	tell 诉 tell
事先	shìxiān	副	beforehand; in advance
口头	kǒutóu	形	oral
书面	shūmiàn	形	written
字样	zìyàng	名	written expressions
单位	dānwèi	名	unit
尊敬	zūnjìng	形/动	Dear (addressing letter); respected 尊 respect 敬 honour
准假	zhǔnjià	动	authorize leave or absence 准 allow
敬礼	jìnglǐ	动	salute; yours sincerely(ending letter), extend greetings
将	jiāng	副	will, about to, be going to
就业	jiùyè	动/名	get a job; employment
层	céng	量	floor; layer
就座	jiùzuò	动	be seated, take one's seat

| 学生会 | xuéshēnghuì | 名 | student union |

 对话2 Dialogue Two

小王：小李，你的中文好，快看看墙上写的是什么？

小李：好像是一个通知。

小王：是关于什么的通知？

小李：音乐讲座的。

小王：你知道通知和通告有什么不同吗？

小李：都差不多，不过通告比通知更加正式一点儿。

小王：通告是不是比通知更大一点儿？

小李：<u>就范围而言</u>④，对。因为通知大多是对内的，通告是对外的。

小王：怪不得我经常听人说这是内部通知，不公开。

小李：没错儿。

小王：可以说通告就是公开的通知吗？

小李：可以这么说。

小王：哎，你还知道通告和广告的区别吗？

小李：广告就是<u>广而告之</u>⑤的意思，是为商业服务的。电视上天天都有。

小王：那公告呢？

小李：就是公开告诉你呀！

课文 Text

怎样写请假条和通知

过去,当你有急事不能去上班或者上课时,你需要写张请假条请假。现在大家一般都发邮件或者短信请假。但不管使用哪种方式,你都要写清楚你是谁、跟谁请假、请假的原因和请假多长时间。

如果你有活动需要事先告诉参加的人员,你可以用两种方法通知他们。一种方法是口头告诉他们,这叫做口头通知。另一种方法是用文字告诉他们,这叫做书面通知。写书面通知时要写清楚时间、地点、事情和参加人员,最后要写上发通知的单位和日期。你还可以在"通知"前面加上"重要"、"紧急"等字样,以引起人们的注意。请看下例。

请假条

尊敬的黄老师：

今天我病了,拉肚子,不能来上课了,非常抱歉。请求老师准假一天。

此致

敬礼

你的学生 李贵

十月十六日

通知

　　五月四日星期三下午，京华商学院的于院长将来我校做关于就业问题的专题讲座。讲座将于下午两点正式开始，请有兴趣的同学于两点以前到五号楼二层大教室就座。

学生会
四月二十二日

语法注释 Grammar Notes

① 没想到 – didn't expect that...

For example:

我没想到他会来。
I didn't expect that he would come.

② 谁知道呢！– Who knows! It is an expression to convey a sense of uncertainty on the part of the speaker, often with 呢 at the end. It often implies that the speaker is not in a position to help or is not very keen on the subject being discussed.

③ 要不要我替你写？– 替…V… "for" or "on behalf of" someone do something.

For example:

(1) 他现在太忙，我替他去吧？
He's too busy at present. Shall I go instead of him?

(2) 我有点感冒，你能替我买点药吗？
I've got a touch of flu. Can you buy some medicine for me?

④ 就范围而言 – 就……而言 is a phrase meaning "in terms of" ... or "as far as...is concerned". It is a formal way to draw the listener's attention to an item the speaker would like to stress.

> **For example:**
> (1) 就我而言，我觉得他这么说没什么。
> Personally speaking, I don't have any problem with him saying that.
> (2) 就这件事而言，我们都认为是你的不对。
> As far as this matter is concerned, we all think that it is your fault.

⑤ 广而告之 – make it known widely. This is based on a classical construction. 而 ("and") is a function word linking clauses, while 之 "it" usually functions as an object substitute for something referred to earlier on.

文化知识 Cultural Note

病假和事假

As elsewhere, if you fall sick and can't go to work in China, you are expected to submit a sick note from a doctor either before or after the absence. In schools, a note from parents or at university a note from students themselves (who are adults after all) will do for short absence for a day or two. In addition, there is another type of leave, similar to unpaid leave in Britain, which is sometimes called "leave of absence" (事假) or leave approved on compassionate grounds. It is usually approved when the applicant has a specific reason, often for personal. However, such leave could affect the performance assessment of the individual concerned.

练习 Exercises

口语练习 Speaking Practice

小组活动

A. 你有事不能去参加一个事先定好的活动。你请一位同学把你的情况转告 (inform, pass on information) 大家；

B. 你把 A 请假的理由转告给 C；

C. 你转告给 D……N；

请 N 把 A 请假的原因告诉大家。

大家看看他说得对不对。如果不对，找出是谁把话传错了？

听力练习 Listening Practice

Listen to the following dialogues and choose the correct answer for each question.

1) a. 他有病　　　　b. 他很忙　　　　c. 他是一半中国人
2) a. 读书　　　　　b. 锻炼身体　　　c. 看电视
3) a. 八点　　　　　b. 九点　　　　　c. 十点
4) a. 他病了　　　　b. 他要看球赛　　c. 他没有做完作业
5) a. 她拉肚子了　　b. 她头疼　　　　c. 她妈妈来了
6) a. 在医院里　　　b. 在家里　　　　c. 在学校里
7) a. 他头疼　　　　b. 他腿疼　　　　c. 他感冒了
8) a. 他打电话给老师　b. 老师给他打电话　c. 王为给他打电话

语法练习 Grammar Practice

1. 多项选择

1) 他做了坏事，你怎么还 _____ 他说话？
   　a. 给　　　　　　b. 跟　　　　　　c. 替

2) 他今天为什么没有来？你知道 _____ 吗？
   a. 原本　　　　　　b. 原因　　　　　　c. 原来

3) 今天晚上开会，你 _____ 她了吗？
   a. 通知　　　　　　b. 通告　　　　　　c. 通报

4) 这两种字体没有什么 _____。
   a. 区分　　　　　　b. 区别　　　　　　c. 地区

5) 情况很 _____，你们必须马上出发。
   a. 重要　　　　　　b. 紧急　　　　　　c. 紧要

6) 我们应该 _____ 老人，爱护孩子。
   a. 尊敬　　　　　　b. 热爱　　　　　　c. 敬爱

7) 我弟弟从小就很 _____，不管什么东西，他都一学就会。
   a. 听话　　　　　　b. 明白　　　　　　c. 聪明

8) 这儿的空气不 _____，你应该出去走走。
   a. 新鲜　　　　　　b. 清楚　　　　　　c. 干净

2. 选词填空

本来、不管、关于、出去、只好、容易、
正式、范围、非常、以为

　　昨天下午，学校里有一个 ____ 太空的讲座，请了中国第一个太空人杨利伟来讲演。这个讲座 ____ 只对内、不对外，____ 是航天系的高年级学生和老师，可是，秘书小王搞错了，____（mì shū）是对外开放，他把通告贴了 _____（tiē）。通告一贴出，很多人早早就来到了大教室就座。讲座应该在六点半 _____ 开始，可是五点半就已经没有座位了。秘书好不 ____ 才给到会的几位老专家找到了座位。航天系的学生 _____ 站着听了。可是 _____ 是坐着的还是站着的，大家都热情高涨。这次讲座 _____ 成功。

认字识词 Words with Known Characters

1. 查找出下列词语的词义，并翻译成英文。

办法 _____   同事 _____

内科 _____   外科 _____

拉面 _____   地区 _____

签证 _____   笨蛋 _____

笨头笨脑 _____   笨手笨脚 _____

2. 翻译下列词语，并找出其结构规律。请至少再找出五个同样结构的词。

倒茶 _____   洗车 _____

经商 _____   扫地 _____

越级 _____   种菜 _____

打字 _____   放羊 _____

拍电影 _____   生孩子 _____

放火 _____   讲话 _____

翻译练习 Translation

Say the following sentences in Chinese first and then write them out in characters.

1) I don't feel well, can you write a sick note for me?
2) None of us expected that he couldn't speak Chinese.
3) The battery of my mobile phone is flat. I never thought yours would be flat as well. How can we find someone to help us?
4) As far as population is concerned, China is the most populous country in the world.
5) Why is Xiao Wang so formally dressed today?
   Who knows! He's been quite odd recently.
6) I went to Xinjiang（新疆）in the summer and the roast lamb there was really delicious.

阅读 Reading

成语故事 The stories behind Chinese idioms

bēi gōng shé yǐng
杯弓蛇影

从前有个叫乐广的人请朋友到家里喝酒。可是那位朋友喝完酒回家后就生病了。乐广派人去问候他，才知道他怀疑那天他用的酒杯里有条小蛇。酒杯里怎么会有蛇呢？经过仔细观 chá guān 察(observation)，乐广终于(finally)找到了原因。他再次把那位朋友请到家里，还让他坐在上次喝酒的位子上。乐广给朋友倒了一杯酒，一条小蛇又在杯中出现了。这时候乐广把挂在墙上的弓(bow)取下来，杯中的小蛇也就不见了。原来，挂在墙上的那张弓的影子倒映(reflected)在酒杯里，看起来很像一条小蛇。他朋友恍然大悟(suddenly realized)，病也立刻好了。

实用练习 Module Practice

1) 下个月底学生会要举行新年舞会，请你写一个通知告诉大家。

2) 写一个请假条给你的老师或老板，请假的原因请自己找。

汉字笔顺 Stroke Order

CHINESE IN STEPS 4 *Lesson 36*

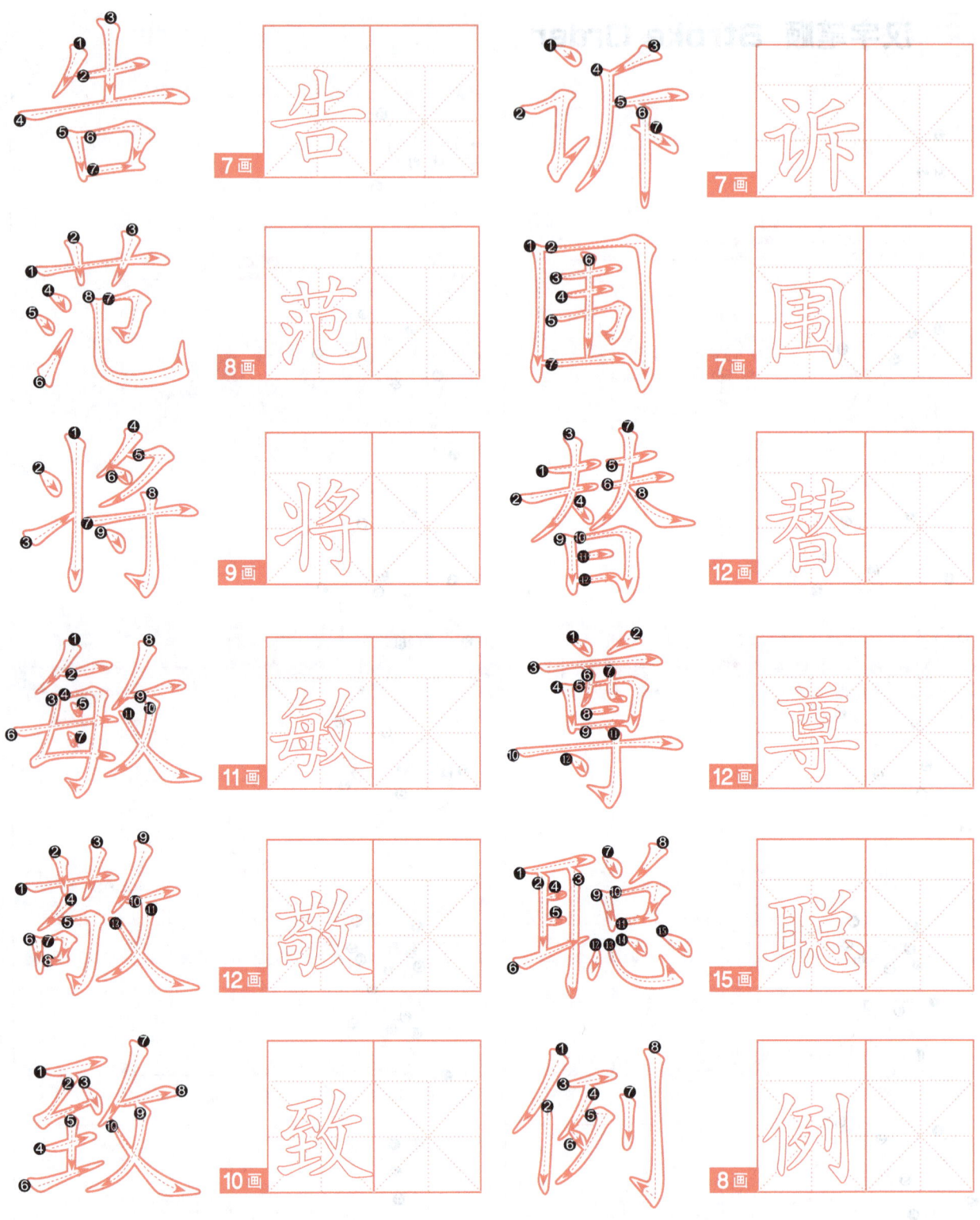

37
第三十七课　写信

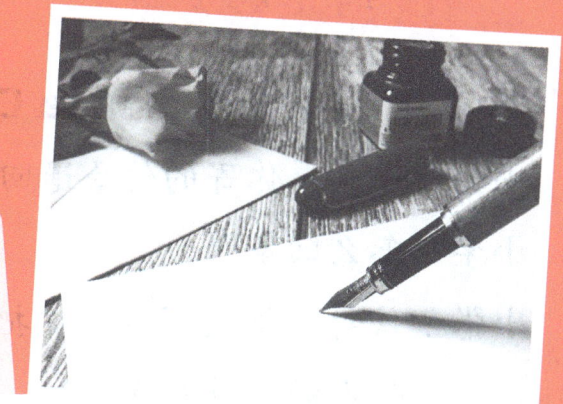

Learning Objectives
To talk about differences and similarities
To read and write Chinese letters
To learn about adverb + verb/adjective construction

🔊 生词 1 New Words

退	tuì	动	send back, return, retreat
信封	xìnfēng	名	envelope 封 seal; m.w for letter
格式	géshì	名	format
相反	xiāngfǎn	形	opposite, contrary 反 opposite; against
啦	la	助	a phrase-final particle (fusion of 了 + 啊)
难道	nándào	副	surely not, do you mean to say
不见得	bújiàndé	副	not necessarily
靠	kào	介/动	alongside; keep to; rely on
例外	lìwài	名	exception
阿拉伯	Ālābó	专名	Arab, Arabic 阿 noun prefix 伯 uncle
表达	biǎodá	动/名	express; expression
日期	rìqī	名	date
辫子	biànzi	名	plaits, pigtail 辫 plaits
袍子	páozi	名	robe
世界	shìjiè	名	world 世 world 界 circles; boundary
多元	duōyuán	形	diversified 元 element, component

八十七　87

对话 1 Dialogue One

小张：小李，你寄的信给退回来了。

小李：怎么回事？

小张：信封的格式不对，你把寄信人、收信人的地址写反了。

小李：写反了？难道是寄信人地址在下，收信人地址在上？

小张：当然啦！

小李：怎么中国这儿什么都是相反的？！

小张：那不见得。

小李：你看，中国开车靠右行，英国开车靠左行。

小张：大部分国家都是靠右行，只有少数几个国家例外。

小李：中国人姓在前，名在后。

小张：阿拉伯国家也是这样。

小李：中国人表达日期从大到小，西方是从小到大。

小张：日本就是从大到小的。

小李：中国男人穿裙子，留辫子。

小张：真的？我怎么没看见？你是在哪儿看见的？

小李：在电影里。

小张：我说呢。不过那不是裙子，那是袍子。

小李：那留辫子是怎么回事[①]？

小张：现在不是有很多男人也留辫子吗？世界是多元的。

生词 2 New Words

亲爱的	qīnàide	形	dear (intimate form of address); darling 亲 next of kin; kiss
一切	yíqiè	代	everything, all 切 be close to; cut
挂念	guàniàn	动	worry about; miss
语音	yǔyīn	名	pronunciation; voice
语调	yǔdiào	名	intonation 调 intonation, tone
错误	cuòwù	名	mistake, error 误 error
收获	shōuhuò	名/动	gains, harvest 获 capture, reap
全部	quánbù	副/名	completely, all 全 whole, complete
讲课	jiǎngkè	动	give a lecture, teach
一开始	yìkāishǐ	副	at the beginning
吃力	chīlì	形	strenuous, require great effort
习惯	xíguàn	动/名	get used to; habit 惯 spoil; be used to
居住	jūzhù	名/动	habitation; live 居 live
条件	tiáojiàn	名	conditions
同学	tóngxué	名	classmate, schoolmate
食物	shíwù	名	food 食 food; eat
火锅	huǒguō	名	hot pot 锅 pot
狗不理包子	Gǒubùlǐbāozi	专名	a well known brand of steamed bun in Tianjin
附上	fùshàng	动	attach 附 add, attach
好客	hàokè	形	be hospitable 好 like, love
伙伴	huǒbàn	名	partner 伙 mate 伴 companion
于爱华	Yúàihuá	专名	a name
误以为	wùyǐwéi	动	mistaken for; mistakenly believe
如此	rúcǐ	副	be like this; so, such
祝	zhù	动	wish
健康	jiànkāng	形/名	healthy; health 康 healthy

课文 Text

亲爱的高老师：

　　您好！时间过得真快，我们来中国已经一个月了。这里的一切都很好，请不要挂念。

　　我们现在每周上十八个小时的课。我们有六七门课，我最喜欢的是口语课和语法课。你知道我的语音语调不太好，语法的错误也很多，上这两门课我的收获很大。这里的老师全部都用汉语讲③课，一开始我感到非常吃力，现在我已经习惯了。

　　我现在住在学校留学生宿舍里，这里的居住条件非常好，跟大饭店差不多。房间里有电视和空调，每天还有服务员来打扫房间，我都给惯坏了。学校的餐厅也很不错，不过北京的食物非常便宜，我常常和同学出去吃饭。我很喜欢吃火锅和狗不理包子。

　　来北京前您告诉③我们北京又大又漂亮，可是我没有想到北京有这么大，这么漂亮！附上几张照片，这是我和李健在校园里拍的。我们还没有好好出去玩过②。

　　中国人很好客，我已经交了不少朋友。我还有一个语言伙伴，她叫于爱华，是英语系的学生。很多人误以为她是我女朋友。不过我倒是希望如此④，因为她人很好，长得又非常漂亮。关于她我有很多要对您说③的，今天就写到这儿吧。我还要准备明天的听写呢。

　　等着您的回信。祝您身体健康！

　　　　　　　　　　　　　　　　　　　　您的学生　王京

　　　　　　　　　　　　　　　　　　　　2019.3.25

语法注释 Grammar Notes

①那留辫子是怎么回事？– 怎么回事 "How come?" "What's it all about?" is a colloquial expression asking for the details or reasons, possibly with a sense of emphasis.

> **For example:**
> (1) 你腰疼是怎么回事？
> How come you have backache?
> (2) 你昨天没去上班，怎么回事？
> How come you didn't go to work yesterday?

②我们还没有好好出去玩过。– 好好 means "really" or "properly" here, but it also has a more literal meaning of "nicely".

> **For example:**
> (1) 这本书你要好好（地）看一下。
> You should take a proper look at this book.
> (2) 这件事你得好好地跟他说。
> You must talk to him properly about this.

③告诉，说，讲 – note the differences among them in terms of usage as below:

> **For example:**
> (1) 他告诉我老王去北京了。
> He told me Lao Wang had gone to Beijing.
> (2) 他说老王去北京了。
> He said Lao Wang had gone to Beijing.
> (3) 她讲课时说老王去北京了。
> When she was teaching she said Lao Wang had gone to Beijing.

④希望如此 – It is a common expression, meaning "I hope so".

文化知识 Cultural Note

狗不理包子

狗不理包子 is a well known brand of steamed bun with stuffing. It originated from Tianjin. The name of the brand doesn't sound very elegant, but there's a story behind it. It goes like this: Over a hundred years ago, there was a young boy nicknamed 狗不理 by his parents because of his strong character. 狗不理 literally means that even dogs take no notice. But the boy later turned out to be a master chef who cooked really delicious 包子. Due to his nickname, his 包子 was referred to as 狗不理包子 and the name soon travelled far beyond the city of Tianjin. It is said that the Empress Dowager Cixi（慈禧太后）liked 狗不理包子 so much that she ordered more to be sent to her after she had a taste of them.

练习 Exercises

口语练习 Speaking Practice

小组活动

1. 介绍你们国家写信和写信封的格式。
2. 介绍你们国家开车和穿衣的习惯。

听力练习 Listening Practice

Listen to the following dialogues and choose the correct answer for each question.

1) a. 他们是律师　　　b. 他们是中文老师　　c. 他们是工人
2) a. 山东　　　　　　b. 山西　　　　　　　c. 广东
3) a. 以为他脑子坏了　b. 以为他感冒了　　　c. 以为他被人卖了
4) a. 马、茶　　　　　b. 吗、草　　　　　　c. 妈、菜
5) a. 包裹　　　　　　b. 明信片　　　　　　c. 信
6) a. 他自己　　　　　b. 朋友王京　　　　　c. 他的妈妈
7) a. 寄信人地址在上　b. 收信人地址在下　　c. 收信人地址在上
8) a. 地址写反了　　　b. 没有邮票　　　　　c. 邮票价钱不对

语法练习 Grammar Practice

1. 多项选择

1) 在这时候，我很难用语言 _____ 我的感情。
   a. 表示　　　　　b. 表现　　　　　　c. 表达

2) 他 _____ 比你高多少。
   a. 不怎么　　　　b. 不由得　　　　　c. 不见得

3) 这个星期我们很忙，大家都得来上班，谁也不 _____ ！
   a. 里外　　　　　b. 例外　　　　　　c. 除外

4) 他们以为圣诞节可以好好休息一下，结果正好 _____，他们的经理叫他们圣诞节加班。
   a. 相当　　　　b. 相近　　　　c. 相反

5) 在信里，他给他妈妈 _____ 了几张自己的照片。
   a. 附上　　　　b. 寄上　　　　c. 送上

6) 你要抓住 _____ 机会医好他。
   a. 一样　　　　b. 一般　　　　c. 一切

7) 吸烟是一种坏 _____。
   a. 爱好　　　　b. 习惯　　　　c. 常事

8) 好久没有收到你的信了，爸爸很 _____ 你。
   a. 挂念　　　　b. 想着　　　　c. 着想

2. 选词填空

到、还是、怎么、问、就是、别人、一点儿、
后来、时候、吹

我刚到上海的 _____，因为不懂上海话，出了不少笑话。我 _____ 理发馆去刮脸洗头，理发师 _____ 我："修面吗？"我问他："别人都修吗？"他说："_____ 都修。"我说："好吧，那我也修吧。"理发师就为我刮了脸。_____ 他又问我："打头吗？"我想："他 _____ 要打我？"我就问他："你只打我一个人，_____ 来这里的顾客都打呀？"他说："通通都打。"我想："通通都打是这里的规定，那我也打吧！"就这样，理发师给我洗了头，_____ 了风，完了拿过镜子一照说："好了！"我说："好啦？你怎么不打我了？""已经打过了。"理发师说。"打过了？怎么 _____ 不疼啊？"原来，在上海话里，修面就是刮脸，打头 _____ 洗头。

认字识词 Words with Known Characters

1. 查找出下列词语的词义，并翻译成英文。

退休	_____	反对	_____
误会	_____	反义词	_____
错误	_____	同义词	_____
靠近	_____	同音词	_____
附件	_____	老伴儿	_____

2. 翻译下列词语，并找出其结构规律。请至少再找出五个同样结构的词。

干洗	_____	慢跑	_____
高考	_____	大选	_____
巧遇	_____	冷烫	_____
单打	_____	双打	_____
早婚	_____	晚婚	_____
紧靠	_____	白吃	_____

翻译练习 Translation

Say the following sentences in Chinese first and then write them out in characters.

1) Yesterday at Laowang's house I saw a picture of his grandfather wearing a gown and pigtail.
2) There are no buses on the road this morning. Do you know what is happening?
3) I couldn't quite understand the accent (口音) of the people there at the beginning, but I have now got used to it.
4) What did you say? Surely he did not drive on the left this morning on his way to work?
5) This is a diverse world. In some countries, a man can have as many wives as he likes.
6) I lived in South Africa for 5 years and made a lot of friends there.

阅读 Reading

成语故事 The stories behind Chinese idioms

狐假虎威
hú jiǎ hǔ wēi

一天，老虎(tiger)觉得肚子饿了，就到外面去找吃的东西。当它走到一片森林(sēn lín)(forest)时，看到前面有只狐狸(hú li)(fox)。它觉得这正是个好机会，就扑(pū)(jump)过去把狐狸抓住了。

狐狸看见自己跑不掉了，就对老虎说："你怎么敢吃我？我是动物之王！"老虎当然不相信。狐狸马上接着说："你要是不信，就跟在我后面去森林里走一走，看看动物见了我是不是都会逃走。"老虎答应了。于是，它们一起向森林深处走去。狐狸在前面走，老虎在后面跟着。果然(guǒ rán)（as expected），森林里大大小小的动物看见老虎非常害怕，马上都跑掉了。老虎不知道这些动物是怕自己，以为它们是怕狐狸，所以就把狐狸放了。

实用练习 Module Practice

从下列两个题目中任意选择一个题目作答。

1. 给你的家人写一封信，字数为250到300个汉字。问候他们、告诉他们你的学习或工作情况，请他们不要挂念你。

2. 给你的新语言伙伴写一封邮件。告诉他/她你在哪儿看到他/她找语言伙伴的广告，介绍一下你自己，和他/她商量语言交换的时间和地点。

汉字笔顺 Stroke Order

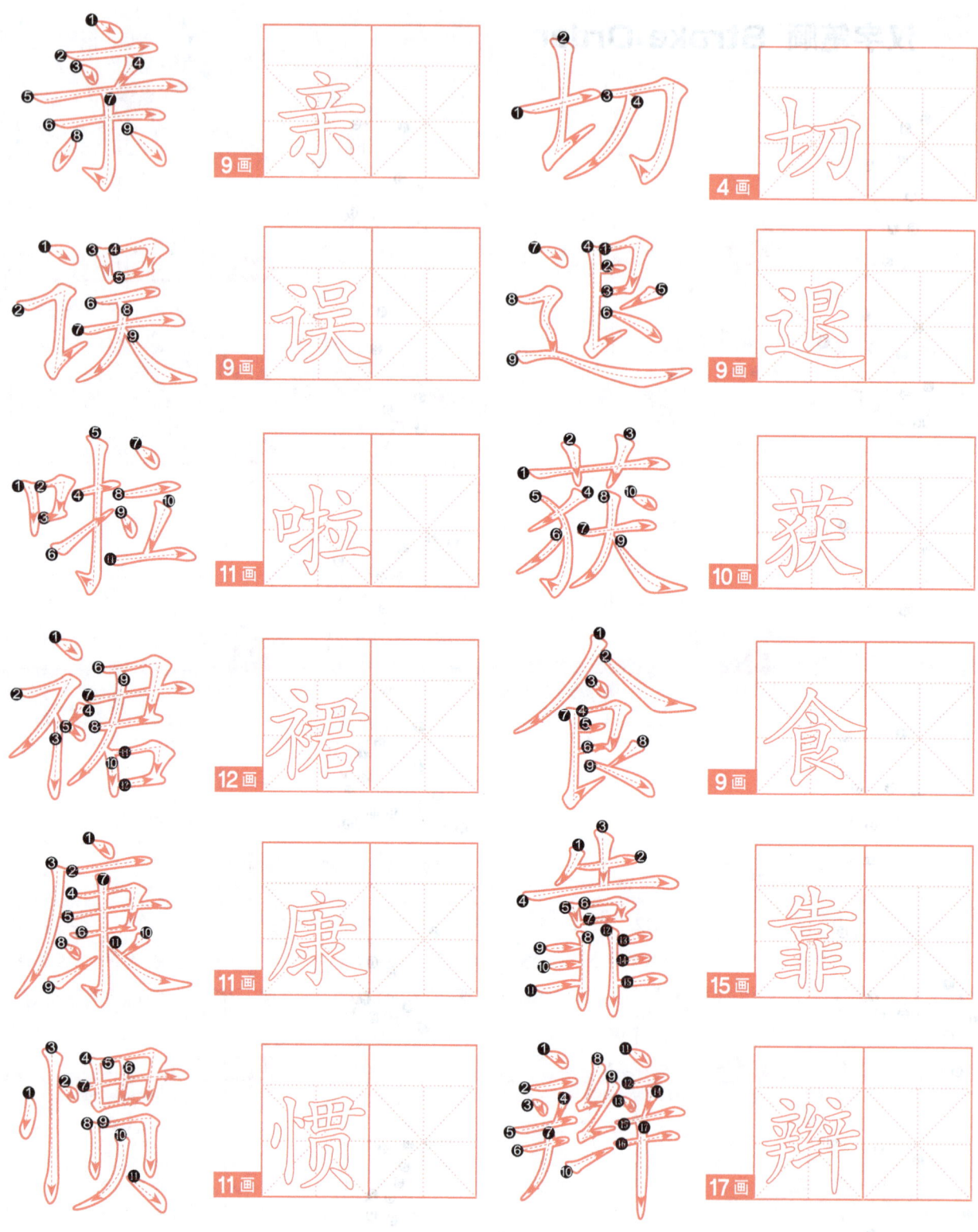

38
第三十八课　申请工作

Learning Objectives
To write a covering letter
To write your curriculum vitae
To learn about the doer + verb construction

🔊 生词 1 New Words

招聘	zhāopìn	动	recruit 招 recruit; attract 聘 invite to engage
实习	shíxí	动/名	do intern work; work experience 实 actual, real
实习生	shíxíshēng	名	intern
有意者	yǒuyìzhě	名	person who is interested 意 desire 者 person
工资	gōngzī	名	salary
求职信	qiúzhíxìn	名	job application letter
面试	miànshì	名	interview
居然	jūrán	副	unexpectedly
牛皮大王	niúpídàwáng	名	(colloquial) braggart
才华	cáihuá	名	talent 才 talent 华 glamour
出众	chūzhòng	形	outstanding 众 mass
精通	jīngtōng	动/形	be proficient in 精 perfect; accuracy
夸张	kuāzhāng	形/动	exaggerating; exaggerate 夸 boast; praise
推销	tuīxiāo	动	promote; market 推 push 销 sale
老王卖瓜，自卖自夸			to blow one's own trumpet
以（……能力）		介	with (...the ability of) 能力 ability, capability

对话 1 Dialogue One

于爱华：小王，你不是要找个公司实习吗？你看看这个广告。

王　京：招聘实习生，每周工作六小时。有意者请发简历来。

于爱华：工资很高，每小时五十块。

王　京：我马上跟他们联系。

于爱华：你需要准备一封求职信和一份中文简历，还要准备面试。

王　京：我这儿有一份中文简历，你帮我看看，好不好？

于爱华：好。……小王，没想到你居然①是个牛皮大王！

王　京：你说什么？！我哪儿吹了？

于爱华："才华出众，精通汉语等五国语言"。

王　京：这不是吹牛，只是有点儿夸张。

于爱华：不是有点儿，而是太夸张了。

王　京：不夸张怎么能把自己推销出去？

于爱华：中国人最不喜欢这样的人，老王卖瓜，自卖自夸。

王　京：我是姓王，可是我没有卖瓜。

于爱华：好，你没有卖瓜。你不是精通汉语吗？怎么连这句话也不懂。学语言不学习文化是不行的。

王　京：好，是我错了，我不该吹牛。你帮我改改，好不好？

于爱华：你不怕推销不出去吗？

王　京：不怕。以你的能力、我的资历，推销不出去才怪呢②。

于爱华：啊！你还在吹啊！

🔊 生词 2 New Words

毕业	bìyè	动	graduate 毕 complete
皇家	huángjiā	名	royal family 皇 emperor
苏格兰	Sūgélán	专名	Scotland 苏 revive; a surname 兰 orchid
伦敦欧洲商学院		专名	European Business School London
目前	mùqián	副	at present
主修	zhǔxiū	动	major in
金融	jīnróng	名	finance 融 circulation
副修	fùxiū	动	minor in 副 secondary; deputy, vice
熟悉	shúxī	动/形	be familiar with 悉 know
热情	rèqíng	形/名	enthusiastic; zeal
胜任	shèngrèn	动	capable of, up to the job 胜 victory 任 take a post
传真	chuánzhēn	名	fax 传 pass
信箱	xìnxiāng	名	mailbox
学历	xuélì	名	educational background
至今	zhìjīn	副	up to now 至 to
海德	Hǎidé	专名	Hyde (transliteration)
经历	jīnglì	名/动	experience
建筑	jiànzhù	名/动	architecture, construction 建 build 筑 construct
分行	fēnháng	名	branch
风险	fēngxiǎn	名	risk
技能	jìnéng	名	skill 技 skill
爱好	àihào	名/动	hobby
爬山	páshān	动	climb a mountain, hiking
骑马	qímǎ	动	ride a horse
卡拉OK	kǎlā ok	名	karaoke

课文 Text

求职信

尊敬的周小姐：

　　从报上我看到贵行正在招聘实习生，我对此工作十分感兴趣，特写此信申请。

　　我一直对银行业十分感兴趣。高中毕业后我就到皇家苏格兰银行实习了一年。我现在是伦敦欧洲商学院大二的学生，目前在北京语言大学学习汉语。我主修金融，副修汉语。我会说多种语言，熟悉银行业务，特别是信用卡业务。我<u>为人热情、乐于助人</u>③。我想我一定能胜任这个工作。

　　附上我的简历。请查收。

　　此致

敬礼

求职人 王京

2019 年 5 月 16 日

个人简历

姓名：王京

出生年月：1982年2月7日

国籍：英国

联系地址：北京东城区建国路123号

联系方式：手机电话 13987556398　　　　　传真：010 32986745

电子信箱：daweiwang@yahoo.com.cn

学历：

2001年9月——至今	伦敦欧洲商学院学生
1994年9月——2000年7月	苏格兰金山中学学生
1988年8月——1994年7月	伦敦海德小学学生

工作经历：

2003年9月——至今	家庭英语教师
2000年8月——2001年8月	皇家苏格兰银行实习生
1998年7月——1998年9月	金山建筑公司实习生

工作兴趣：银行风险管理、信用卡业务、私人银行业务

技能：精通计算机；会说四国语言——英语、德语、意大利语、汉语

爱好：爬山、骑马、跳舞、卡拉OK、上网

语法注释 Grammar Notes

① 居然 – an adverbial phrase indicating something unexpected or surprising, can be used together with 没想到.

> **For example:**
> (1) 没想到居然会在这儿见到老同学!
> What a surprise to meet an old classmate here!
> (2) 他居然不打招呼就自己走了。
> How could he leave on his own without telling anyone?

② 推销不出去才怪呢。– "It would be strange if...; it is absolutely impossible that".

> **For example:**
> (1) 她喜欢睡懒觉,这么早,她能起来才怪呢。
> She likes to lie in; it would be strange if she were up so early.
> (2) 如果他再酒后开车,不出事才怪呢。
> If he keeps on drinking and driving, it'll be surprising if he doesn't have an accident.

③ 为人热情、乐于助人 – There are many four character phrases in Chinese, some from proverbs with stories behind them, some idiomatic phrases deriving from a long period of usage. You need to pay close attention to such expressions as they are very typical of the language, and reflect the dichotomous and rhythmic aspects of the Chinese language.

文化知识 Cultural Note

中国人的谦虚

Traditionally, modesty is considered a virtue that a well-educated person should have. Chinese modesty is usually reflected in two ways: one often understates his/her own achievements when talking about himself/herself (nonetheless it doesn't matter to overstate the achievements of others). The other way is that one tends to deflect others' compliments by using what could be seen as a complete denial of the compliments (such as replying 不好, not good, 哪里哪里, not at all). This can often lead to misunderstanding if you are not fully aware of this as part of the Chinese culture. It is such that some Westerners even think that there is little difference between Chinese modesty and lying, and some others (even Chinese people themselves) find it tiring. But for Chinese, this is part of the culture of 礼让. It happens all the time, especially in formal occasions.

练习 Exercises

口语练习 Speaking Practice

小组活动：面试

a. 你是一名求职者，正在接受公司的面试。别忘了，除了回答问题以外，你也应该问些问题，比如工资、住房、公司班车等等。

b. 你是公司的总经理，你正在面试求职者。你要问很多问题，比如工作经历、专业能力等等。

其他人：你们都是公司的高层领导，都正在参与面试新员工。你们每人至少提一个问题。

听力练习 Listening Practice

Listen to the following dialogues and choose the correct answer for each question.

1) a. 不到一年　　　　b. 一年　　　　　　c. 一年多
2) a. 他爸爸让他去　　b. 他没有钱了　　　c. 他要练习汉语
3) a. 朋友很忙　　　　b. 朋友和他说英语　c. 他没有中国朋友
4) a. 他的汉语不好　　b. 他的英语不好　　c. 他的简历不够好
5) a. 十几个人　　　　b. 几十个人　　　　c. 几百个人
6) a. 十几个人　　　　b. 几十个人　　　　c. 几百个人
7) a. 工作少　　　　　b. 学历不够高　　　c. 高不成低不就
8) a. 求职信　　　　　b. 简历　　　　　　c. 名片

语法练习 Grammar Practice

1. 多项选择

1) 伦敦大学正在_____数学讲师，你可以去试试。
   a. 招聘　　　　b. 录取　　　　c. 口试

2) 他本来是个人见人爱的好学生，没想到他_____做出这种事情来。
   a. 居然　　　　b. 突然　　　　c. 虽然

3) 他的女朋友_____电脑，你可以叫她看一看你的电脑有什么毛病。
   a. 普通　　　　b. 精通　　　　c. 打通

4) 他们带了样品，去美国_____他们的产品。
   a. 推行　　　　b. 推销　　　　c. 推卖

5) 所有的外国留学生，毕业以后都可以在英国_____一年。
   a. 练习　　　　b. 实习　　　　c. 学习

6) 就是你把你自己____上天，人们还是不会相信你的。
   a. 说　　　　　b. 告诉　　　　c. 吹

7) 这个工作很重要，你看他能不能____？
   a. 担任　　　　b. 胜任　　　　c. 当

8) 通知发出去已经一个星期了，可是_____还没有人报名。
   a. 今天　　　　b. 今后　　　　c. 至今

2. 选词填空

广告、招聘、精通、马上、居然、熟练、种、使用、看着、没想到

一个公司要_____一名新职员，于是就在报纸上登出一份广告说："招聘文职（clerical）人员，要会打字、懂电脑、____两种语言。符合（meet）条件者机会平等（equal）。"_____第二天，

第一个来应聘（apply）的＿＿＿是一条狗。"对不起，我不能招聘一条狗。"经理说。狗不服气（not convinced），拿出了＿＿＿和他讲理（argue）。经理没有办法，只好问道："你会打字吗？"那条狗＿＿＿走到打字机前打了一封信。"你懂得怎样＿＿＿电脑吗？"经理又问。那条狗又坐在一台电脑前，非常＿＿＿地用起电脑来。经理有点儿急了，"我需要的雇员要会说两＿＿＿语言，你会吗？"那条狗得意地＿＿＿经理说："汪！喵！"

认字识词 Words with Known Characters

1. 查找出下列词语的词义，并翻译成英文。

西瓜 ＿＿＿	建造 ＿＿＿
兰花 ＿＿＿	大众 ＿＿＿
事实 ＿＿＿	高科技 ＿＿＿
传球 ＿＿＿	资本 ＿＿＿
皇上 ＿＿＿	胜利 ＿＿＿

2. 翻译下列词语，并找出其结构规律。请至少再找出五个同样结构的词。

中国造 ＿＿＿	心算 ＿＿＿
口吃 ＿＿＿	自助 ＿＿＿
自主 ＿＿＿	师传 ＿＿＿
手写 ＿＿＿	友爱 ＿＿＿
云游 ＿＿＿	日出 ＿＿＿
笔录 ＿＿＿	鱼死网破 ＿＿＿

翻译练习 Translation

Say the following sentences in Chinese first and then write them out in characters.

1) I didn't expect that he would like to boast so much.
2) I have heard that your company is recruiting interns. I am interested in this.
3) Our teacher is very talented. She draws very well.
4) Last year I went to quite a few places in China. Chinese people are all very warm.
5) What are your hobbies? I like climbing, riding, dancing and reading.
6) I have a lot of experience in banking, and I believe that I am capable of doing the job.

阅读 Reading

成语故事 The stories behind Chinese idioms

买椟(dú)还珠

从前有一个楚国人，他有一颗(kē) (a measure word) 漂亮的珍珠(zhēn zhū) (pearl)。他打算把这颗珍珠卖出去。为了卖个好价钱，他请人做了一个精致(jīng zhì) (elegant) 的盒子（盒子 = 椟）。然后，他将珍珠小心地放进盒子里，拿到市场上去卖。

到市场上不久，有一个人看到了这个盒子，他非常喜欢，出高价将盒子买了下来。可是没走几步他又回来了。楚人以为他后悔(huǐ) (regret) 了要退货(return the product)，可是他走到楚人跟前，将盒子打开，取出里面的珍珠，交给楚人说："先生，您的珍珠忘在盒子里了。"他将珍珠还给了楚人，然后拿着空木盒子走了。

实用练习 Module Practice

1. 写一份你自己的简历

注意：内容要符合实际情况，觉得隐私的信息可以不提供。你可以寄给相关公司求职。

2. 写一封求职信

你最想干什么工作，你就写信求什么职，什么工作都可以。

汉字笔顺 Stroke Order

CHINESE IN STEPS 4 Lesson 38

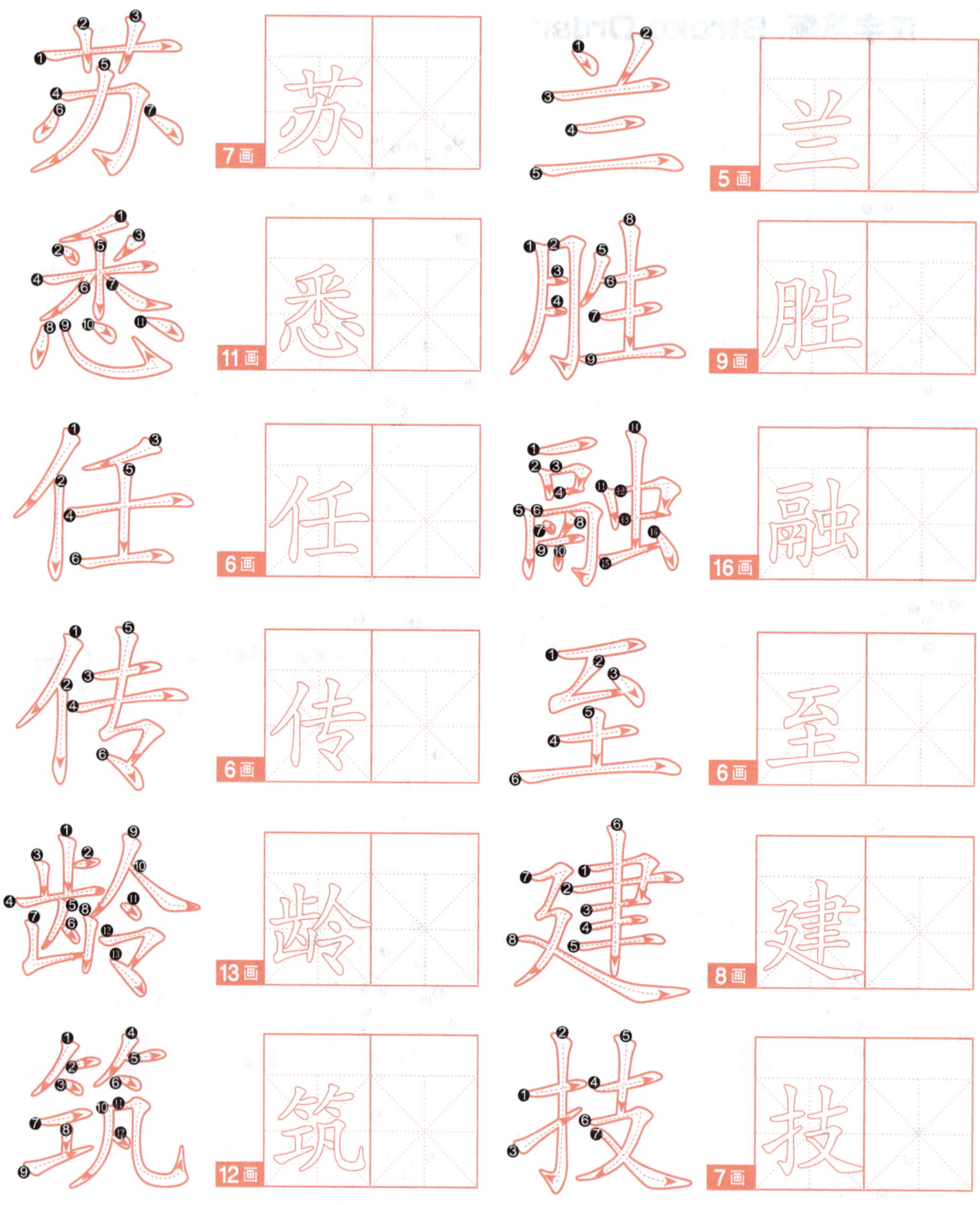

39
第三十九课　购物

Learning Objectives
To talk about shopping and where to shop
To understand bargaining tips and practise
To revise the verb + complement construction formation

🔊 生词 1 New Words

陪	péi	动	accompany
购物	gòuwù	动 + 名	(go) shopping; shopping 购 purchase
逛	guàng	动	walk around (shops), ramble, stroll
淘宝	Táobǎo	专名	Taobao, Chinese online shopping website 淘 wash 宝 treasure
京东	Jīngdōng	专名	Jingdong, Chinese online shopping website
天猫	Tiānmāo	专名	Tmall, Chinese online shopping website
随便	suíbiàn	副/形	casually, casual; as you like 随 follow
牙膏	yágāo	名	toothpaste 膏 paste
牙刷	yáshuā	名	toothbrush; 刷 brush
香皂	xiāngzào	名	toilet soap 皂 soap
肥皂	féizào	名	soap 肥 fat
齐全	qíquán	形	complete 齐 full, complete
与其……不如	yǔqí...bùrú	连	rather…than… 与 with 其 that
必要	bìyào	名/形	necessity; necessary
支付宝	Zhīfùbǎo	专名	Alipay
百货大楼	bǎihuòdàlóu	名	department store
自由市场	zìyóushìchǎng	名	free market
物美价廉	wùměijiàlián	短语	(product) cheap but good 廉 cheap

对话 1 Dialogue One

王京：爱华，我想请你陪我上街购物。

爱华：现在谁还去商店买东西，大家都在淘宝网和京东网上买。

王京：有时候网上看到的和实际的东西不一样。

爱华：不一样可以退货啊。网上的东西很齐全，而且比商店里的东西便宜多了。

王京：那我们上网看看吧。淘宝和京东哪个比较好？

爱华：都差不多。你要买什么？

王京：随便看看，看到什么好就买什么。

爱华：牙膏、牙刷、香皂、肥皂你都买齐了吗？

王京：与其说是买齐了，不如说是带齐了。这些东西我都是从英国带来的。

爱华：天啊，有这个必要吗！

王京：我用惯了西方的牌子，怕在中国买不到。

爱华：要买国外的品牌，你可以上天猫网。天猫和淘宝都可以用支付宝付款。

王京：我听说过支付宝，可是我还没有注册呢。

爱华：那我们今天就去百货大楼吧。

王京：北京的自由市场怎么样？东西多不多？

爱华：多！那里要什么有什么，而且物美价廉。

王京：**那我们还等什么**①，去自由市场！

🔊 补充词汇 Additional Vocabulary

专卖店	zhuānmàidiàn	speciality store	帽子	màozi	hat, cap
礼品店	lǐpǐndiàn	gift shop	手套	shǒutào	gloves
精品店	jīngpǐndiàn	boutique	围巾	wéijīn	scarf, muffler
眼镜店	yǎnjìngdiàn	optician's	高跟鞋	gāogēnxié	high-heel shoes
网店	wǎngdiàn	online shop	休闲装	xiūxiánzhuāng	casual dress
实体店	shítǐdiàn	physical store	晚礼服	wǎnlǐfú	evening wear

🔊 生词 2 New Words

帅哥	shuàigē	名	handsome man
牛仔裤	niúzǎikù	名	jeans 仔 cub; child
洞	dòng	名	hole
故意	gùyì	副	intentionally 故 intentionally; cause; old
骗	piàn	动	cheat, deceive
装	zhuāng	动	put; hold
狗熊	gǒuxióng	名	black bear; a coward
毛裤	máokù	名	long woollen underpants
单裤	dānkù	名	unlined trousers; single layer of outer trousers
过冬	guòdōng	动	spend winter, go through winter
必须	bìxū	情动	must, have to 须 must
暖气	nuǎnqì	名	central heating
美女	měinǚ	名	beautiful woman
羊毛	yángmáo	名	wool
长裙	chángqún	名	long skirt
超短裙	chāoduǎnqún	名	mini skirt
连衣裙	liányīqún	名	dress
追	zhuī	动	court; chase, pursue
优惠价	yōuhuìjià	名	preferential/special price 优 excellent 惠 benefit
打折	dǎzhé	动	give discount 折 discount; fold, break
阿姨	āyí	名	aunt, term of address for a woman similar in age to one's parents 姨 aunt

走神	zǒushén	动	be distracted or absent minded, not concentrating
连忙	liánmáng	副	hurriedly
当场	dāngchǎng	副	on the spot, there and then
死去活来	sǐqùhuólái	短语	hovering between life and death, very much
骂	mà	动	swear at, curse
千万	qiānwàn	副	absolutely, definitely, be sure to, must

对话 2 Dialogue Two

阿姨：帅哥，你需要一条新牛仔裤了。

王京：阿姨②，你搞错了，我裤子上的洞是故意弄破的。

阿姨：我知道，这已经不是最新款式了。

王京：不会吧，我来北京前刚买的。

阿姨：我不会骗你的，你看，这才是现在流行的款式。

爱华：这款式不错，肥肥大大的，里面能装一头狗熊。

阿姨：天气冷了，里面加条毛裤正好。

王京：我只穿单裤，从来没穿过毛裤。

阿姨：看来你还没在北京过过冬，北京这儿冬天冷得很，必须穿毛裤⑤。

爱华：有暖气，没关系。

阿姨：美女，你也买条羊毛长裙吧，这超短裙过不了冬。

爱华：阿姨，羊毛长裙太贵了，我买不起。

阿姨：瞧你说的，你有个外国男朋友，怎么会买不起！

王京：阿姨，她还不是我的女朋友。

阿姨：那就快追！来，这条连衣裙昨天刚到，她穿正好。

王京：真漂亮！我们要了。

爱华：不行不行，价格太贵了！给个优惠价吧？

阿姨：好，我打八折卖给你们③，谁叫我一见到你们就喜欢呢④！

王京：谢谢阿姨。

  课文 Text

"东西"这东西真是个怪"东西"

学习"东西"那一课时，我走神了。后来老师问我知道不知道怎么用"东西"一词。我说："当然知道。我们可以说桌子是'东西'，可是不能说'你是东西'或者'我是东西'，因为我们都不是'东西'。"老师一听，急了，忙说："不对，不对，不能说'我不是东西'。"我连忙说："啊，对不起，你是东西。"老师说："也不能说'你是东西'。"我一听也急了："那你到底是什么东西？"老师当场气得半死，同学们乐得死去活来。

现在我知道了，"你不是东西"是骂人的话，"你是什么东西"也是骂人的话。"东西"这东西真是个怪"东西"，使用"东西"这个词时可得千万小心哪。

语法注释 Grammar Notes

① 那我们还等什么？– Then what are we waiting for? It means "don't wait, here we go".

② 阿姨 – Honorifics such as this are common in Chinese but vary from place to place in terms of when and with whom to use it. This term is similar to 大妈 and tends to be used to address women similar or younger than your own parents.

③ 我打八折卖给你们 – 打八折 is a 20% discount, 七折 30% etc; 50% can be expressed as 打五折 or 打对折.

一百一十七

④ 谁叫我一见到你们就喜欢呢？– "I couldn't help liking you at first sight." It is framed as a rhetorical question ("Who made me like you at first sight?"), and is often used to express the idea that it is someone's own responsibility for what happens. 呢 is often used at the end.

> **For example:**
> (1) 谁叫你不去呢，那儿好玩极了。
> Why didn't you go? It was great there.
> (2) 谁叫他不仔细一点呢，他应该考上的。
> Why wasn't he a bit more careful? He should have passed.

⑤ 必须穿毛裤 – must, have to

> **For example:**
> (1) 明天有雨，去旅游的同学都必须带上雨衣。
> It is going to rain tomorrow. Those students who are traveling must bring raincoats.
> (2) 你到北京时，必须去秀水街逛逛。
> You must go to see Xiushui Street while you are in Beijing.

文化知识 Cultural Note

北方冬天人们的着装

Generally speaking, winter is freezing cold and windy in northern China. Temperatures can be as cold as minus 20 degree centigrade, so people do need to wrap This is themselves up warm. This is why 毛裤 or even 棉裤 (cotton padded trousers) are common winter clothing. Padded jackets are most common, especially those padded with feathers (羽绒服), which have virtually replaced the traditional cotton padded ones (棉袄).

Today new fibres are used for underwear, often called 中空棉 or 保暖裤 . However, with the influence of the West, it is becoming increasingly common that the young generation brave the cold winter just wearing a shirt or a dress. Chinese often joke about this as having 风度 (fashionable style) at the expense of 温度 (temperature).

练习 Exercises

口语练习 Speaking Practice

角色扮演

1) A：你是顾客，正在大商场里随便逛逛。

   B：你是售货员，你要设法卖件衣服给他/她。

2) A：你是顾客，要在自由市场讨价还价，买一件你喜欢的商品。

   B：你是卖东西的店主，你要设法多卖几块钱。

听力练习 Listening Practice

Listen to the following dialogues and choose the correct answer for each question.

1) a. 三千　　　　　　b. 二千　　　　　　c. 一千
2) a. 有工作　　　　　b. 有女朋友　　　　c. 要去女朋友家过年
3) a. 女朋友的爸妈　　b. 他爸妈　　　　　c. 他女朋友
4) a. 太贵了　　　　　b. 钱包不见了　　　c. 没有合适的
5) a. 昨天　　　　　　b. 刚才　　　　　　c. 出门的时候
6) a. 他像个小偷　　　b. 他跟随他们　　　c. 他在跑
7) a. 他不是小偷　　　b. 他跑掉了　　　　c. 他是警察的朋友
8) a. 他抓住了小偷　　b. 他报告了警察　　c. 他告诉了王力

语法练习 Grammar Practice

1. 多项选择

1) 你爸爸妈妈来看你,你应该 _____ 他们好好玩几天。
   a. 陪　　　　　　b. 跟　　　　　　c. 同

2) 我们现在 _____ 吃点儿点心,等会儿一起到饭店里去吃饭。
   a. 顺便　　　　　b. 方便　　　　　c. 随便

3) 你为什么 _____ 跟我过不去呢?
   a. 故意　　　　　b. 好意　　　　　c. 乐意

4) 这几天我忙得 _____。
   a. 不得了　　　　b. 了不得　　　　c. 了不起

5) 你问问他有没有 _____ 这样做。
   a. 必须　　　　　b. 必要　　　　　c. 必然

6) 我见他进来, _____ 站起来打招呼。
   a. 连接　　　　　b. 连连　　　　　c. 连忙

7) 路上车子很多,你得多加 _____。
   a. 小心　　　　　b. 留心　　　　　c. 信心

8) 你不要 _____ 我,这件事的真相我早都知道了。
   a. 听　　　　　　b. 骗　　　　　　c. 信

2. 选词填空

没有、一、与其、可是、不必、每年、也、过、还是、快

　　圣诞节 _____ 到了,这是我在中国过的第一个圣诞节, _____ 是我第一次离开老家伦敦、离开亲人、在外一个人 _____ 圣诞节。我很想念远在英国的亲人。_____ 这个时候,人们都在忙着准备过节的礼物。_____ 到周末,牛津街到处都是人。大公司,小商店, _____ 一家不是人山人海的。虽然北京这里也开始了圣诞销售, _____ 比起伦敦来,这里冷清多了,因为中国人不过圣诞节。

我在这里没有很多朋友，所以今年____准备很多礼物，要买的也早已买好了。可是周末我____想到王府井大街去逛逛。____说是去买东西，倒不如说是去找找感觉。

👁 认字识词 Words with Known Characters

1. 查找出下列词语的词义，并翻译成英文。

故事 _____	陪同 _____
理由 _____	骗子 _____
鞋刷 _____	廉价 _____
随和 _____	购买 _____
随身听 _____	药膏 _____

2. 翻译下列词语，并找出其结构规律。请至少再找出五个同样结构的词。

改变 _____	说明 _____
放大 _____	完成 _____
识破 _____	拉平 _____
表明 _____	推进 _____
刷新 _____	洗净 _____
登高 _____	跌倒 _____

翻译练习 Translation

Say the following sentences in Chinese first and then write them out in characters.

1) After having been cheated by him a few times, we no longer believe whatever he says.
2) In January many shops in the UK sell their goods at a discount.
3) My parents like to go shopping at free markets as the things there are good and cheap.
4) We must meet up next week. Should I go to your place or you come to mine?
5) She intentionally bought this big size dress as she was told it would be the fashion this summer.
6) She is the most beautiful girl in our school and there are lots of boys chasing her.

阅读 Reading

成语故事 The stories behind Chinese idioms

wàng méi zhǐ kě
望 梅 止 渴

有一年夏天，曹操(cáo cāo) (a famous leader in the Three Kingdoms period) 带兵(bīng) (soldiers) 去打仗。这天天气特别热，到了中午，大家都渴得不得了，所以越走越慢。

曹操心里很着急。可是到哪儿去找水呢？他把向导(guide) 找来，小声(low voice) 地问他："这附近有没有水？"向导说："泉(spring) 水在山的那一边，要过去得走好几个小时。"曹操想了一下说："不行，时间来不及(jí)。"他看了看前边的树林(shù lín) (woods)，回头对向导说："你什么也别说，我来想办法。"他骑马跑到队伍前面，大声对士兵(shì bīng)说："士兵们，我知道前面有一大片梅(méi) (plum) 林，那里的梅子又大又好吃，我们快点赶路，过了这个山就到梅林了！"士兵们一听，都好像已经吃到了梅子，口水(saliva) 都流了出来，脚步(foot steps) 也就加快了许多。

实用练习 Module Practice

1. 你想让你朋友帮你买一样东西。你给他/她写一条短信，说明你要的东西的大小、款式、价格、颜色等等。

2. 写一篇短文，介绍一件商品。字数在200字左右。

CHINESE IN STEPS 4 Lesson 39

汉字笔顺 Stroke Order

CHINESE IN STEPS 4　　Lesson 40

40
第四十课　故宫

Learning Objectives
To talk about sightseeing and trips
To learn the written style and the use of 所 plus verb
To learn about the word formation: acronym

🔊 生词 1　New Words

同志	tóngzhì	名	comrade　志 ideal, will
故宫	Gùgōng	专名	The Forbidden City　故 old　宫 palace
博物馆	bówùguǎn	名	museum　博 vast, extensive
参观	cānguān	动	visit and tour around (a place)　观 look, observe
天安门	Tiān'ānmén	专名	Tian'anmen　安 peace
通票	tōngpiào	名	multiple-venue ticket
人民大会堂	Rénmíndàhuìtáng	专名	The Great Hall of the People　堂 hall
停止	tíngzhǐ	动	stop　止 stop
外宾	wàibīn	名	foreign guest
来访	láifǎng	动	come on a visit　访 visit
总理	zǒnglǐ	名	premier, prime minister
举行	jǔxíng	动	hold, take place　举 hold up
宴会	yànhuì	名	banquet　宴 formal meal, banquet
毛主席	Máozhǔxí	专名	Chairman Mao　主 main　席 seat
纪念堂	jìniàntáng	名	memorial hall
仪式	yíshì	名	rite, ceremony　仪 ceremony; appearance
结束	jiéshù	动	finish, end　束 tie, control

126　一百二十六

对话 1 Dialogue One

王小明：同志，我买一张故宫博物院的门票。

售票员：60块一张。

王小明：听说学生优惠，这是我的学生证。

售票员：对，学生票20块一张。

王小明：我还想参观天安门和人民大会堂，你们卖不卖通票？

售票员：对不起，我们现在还没有这个业务。

王小明：人民大会堂今天好像停止参观，你知道为什么吗？

售票员：今天有重要外宾来访，总理要在那儿举行欢迎宴会。

王小明：那我还可以参观毛主席纪念堂吗？

售票员：可以，不过得等到欢迎仪式结束之后。

王小明：我先参观故宫，一个小时后出来正好。

售票员：故宫很大，没有两三个小时你出不来①。

王小明：是吗？那我得赶快进去。谢谢。

售票员：不客气。

补充词汇 Additional Vocabulary

颐和园	Yíhéyuán	Summer Palace
北海公园	Běihǎi gōngyuán	Beihai Park
天坛公园	Tiāntán gōngyuán	Temple of Heaven
自然博物馆	Zìrán Bówùguǎn	Natural Museum
历史博物馆	Lìshǐ Bówùguǎn	History Museum
首都博物馆	Shǒudū Bówùguǎn	Capital Museum
禁止照相	jìnzhǐ zhàoxiàng	No photographs

CHINESE IN STEPS 4   Lesson 40

禁止吸烟	jìnzhǐ xīyān	No Smoking
禁止钓鱼	jìnzhǐ diàoyú	No Fishing
请勿喧哗	qǐngwù xuānhuá	Be quiet
请勿入内	qǐngwù rùnèi	No Entry
闲人免进	xiánrén miǎnjìn	Staff Only

🔊 生词 2 New Words

任何	rènhé	代	any 何 which
禁止	jìnzhǐ	动	forbid 禁 forbid
景点	jǐngdiǎn	名	tourist spot 景 scene
格外	géwài	副	especially, exceptionally
紫禁城	Zǐjìnchéng	专名	Forbidden City
皇宫	huánggōng	名	royal palace
皇帝	huángdì	名	emperor 帝 emperor, imperial
称为	chēngwéi	动	be called as 称 call; say
占地	zhàndì	动	occupy an area of 占 occupy
平方米	píngfāngmǐ	名	square metre 米 meter; rice
现存	xiàncún	动	currently existing, surviving
规模	guīmó	名	scale 规 rule 模 pattern
保存	bǎocún	动	preserve
古代	gǔdài	名	ancient times 古 ancient
建筑群	jiànzhùqún	名	cluster of buildings 群 cluster, group
天文学	tiānwénxué	名	astronomy
紫微星	zǐwēixīng	专名	North Star 微 small, tiny
中天	zhōngtiān	名	centre of the cosmos
所在	suǒzài	名	place; place where something exists
所	suǒ	助	archaic written expression with no specific meaning, often omitted nowadays
天帝	tiāndì	名	celestial emperor (Emperor of Heaven)
因而	yīnér	连	thus, therefore

| 真龙天子 | zhēnlóngtiānzǐ | 名 | real son of the dragon (emperor) |
| 禁地 | jìndì | 名 | forbidden place |

对话 2 Dialogue Two

王小明：请问，参观④毛主席纪念堂是在这儿排队吗？

职　员：是。不过你得先去存包。

王小明：我的包里没有什么东西。

职　员：参观纪念堂不准带任何东西②。

王小明：照相机也不能带吗？

职　员：不能。里面禁止照相。

王小明：请问存包处在哪儿？

职　员：在东面儿。你看，好多人在那儿排队。

王小明：这么长的队！我不应该今天来。

职　员：天天都是这样。

王小明：中国人真多。

职　员：北京是重要的旅游城市，旅游景点多，人也格外多。

CHINESE IN STEPS 4   Lesson 40

  课文 Text

故宫

故宫博物院位于北京市中心,是明、清两代的皇宫,先后居住过24位皇帝。明清时故宫博物院叫紫禁城,1925年开始称为故宫。故宫博物院占地七十二万多平方米,有九千多间房屋,是当今世界上现存规模最大、保存最完好的古代皇宫建筑群。

故宫为什么被称为紫禁城呢?原来,中国古代天文学家认为紫微星居于中天,是天帝所在。因而,把天帝所居住的天宫③叫做紫宫。皇帝自称是天帝的儿子,是真龙天子,因而他们所居住的皇宫被称为紫宫。皇宫是禁地,是不能随便进出的,所以又被称为紫禁城。

语法注释 Grammar Notes

① 没有两三个小时你出不来 – "You won't get round in less than two or three hours." Note the use of double negation here.

② 参观纪念堂不准带任何东西。– Note the use of an interrogative with negation indicating inclusiveness; this is the same with the interrogative pronouns 谁、什么 etc.

For example:

(1) 他现在心情不好,任何人都不想见。
He is not very happy at the moment, and does not want to see anyone at all.

(2) 她经常骗人,所以她现在说任何话,大家都不信了。
She's always deceiving people, so nobody believes a word she says now.

③ 天帝所居住的天宫 – Used as a particle, 所 plus a verb creates a more formal written style but without adding any additional meaning to the new construction, (thus it can be omitted).

> **For example:**
> (1) 天帝所居住的天宫 = 天帝居住的天宫
> Heavenly Palace inhabited by the Celestial Emperor.
> (2) 她所说的话、所做的事 = 她说的话、做的事
> That which she says, (and) that which she does.

④ 参观与访问的区别 – 参观 and 访问 are both translated as "visit" in English, but you can see the difference through the Chinese characters. 参观 is mainly visual "see", while 访问 is more oral "see" and "ask". So you can 参观 or 访问 an institution，but you can only 参观 a place and 访问 a friend.

> **For example:**
> (1) 欢迎你们参观/访问我们公司。
> You are welcome to visit our company.
> (2) 欢迎参观我们的校园。
> You are welcome to visit our campus.
> (3) 我明天要去访问一位老作家。
> I am going to pay a visit to an old writer tomorrow.

文化知识 Cultural Note

参观中国的名胜古迹

Most places of historical interest in China need entry tickets (门票). Many such places are actually quite extensive, such as the Ming Tombs (十三陵) in Beijing, which consists of about a dozen different exhibitions, and Zhou Zhuang (周庄) in Suzhou, which is a small village with a number of museums. It is common in China that in the same place of interest, visitors need to buy separate entry tickets for different exhibitions or shows. But more and more places of this kind offer multi-venue tickets. Like anywhere else, it is usually cheaper to get the multi-venue entry ticket.

练习 Exercises

口语练习

小组活动

每人介绍一个你去过或者听说过的中国有意思的地方。如果你什么地方都没去过、也没有听说过，上网查找一个。如果你去过，请告诉大家有关门票等情况。

听力练习 Listening Practice

Listen to the following dialogues and choose the correct answer for each question.

1) a. 骑马　　　　　b. 爬山　　　　　c. 打篮球
2) a. 读书　　　　　b. 参加球赛　　　c. 旅游
3) a. 北海公园　　　b. 故宫　　　　　c. 长城
4) a. 爬长城　　　　b. 看儿子　　　　c. 参观故宫
5) a. 王京会花钱了　b. 王京不计较钱了　c. 王京会当导游了
6) a. 帮助别人　　　b. 要小费　　　　c. 白用别人
7) a. 香港　　　　　b. 上海　　　　　c. 西安
8) a. 同学　　　　　b. 他自己　　　　c. 同学的妹妹

语法练习 Grammar Practice

1. 多项选择

1) 今天下午我们去＿＿＿＿博物馆，好吗？
   a. 访问　　　　　b. 参观　　　　　c. 观光
2) 我们这学期什么时候＿＿＿＿＿＿？
   a. 完成　　　　　b. 结果　　　　　c. 结束
3) 从今天开始，他们公司＿＿＿＿营业。

a. 停止　　　　　　b. 停顿　　　　　　c. 停下

4) 2020年的奥运会将在日本东京＿＿＿＿＿＿。
　　a. 进行　　　　　　b. 举行　　　　　　c. 举起

5) 这儿＿＿＿＿＿＿机动车辆通行。
　　a. 停止　　　　　　b. 阻止　　　　　　c. 禁止

6) 这次运动会的＿＿＿＿＿＿很大。
　　a. 规模　　　　　　b. 规定　　　　　　c. 规格

7) 这儿经常有车辆＿＿＿＿，请你不要在这儿放东西。
　　a. 里外　　　　　　b. 上下　　　　　　c. 进出

8) 从明年开始，＿＿＿＿＿＿人都不准在公共场合吸烟。
　　a. 任何　　　　　　b. 大多数　　　　　c. 不少

2. 选词填空

住下、离开、所在、名称、真的、虽然、
仔细地、写着、因此、由于

　　有一个老外到中国去旅游。当天晚上在旅馆（hostel）＿＿＿＿以后，他想一个人出去逛逛这个城市。他不懂汉语，＿＿＿＿怕迷路(mí lù)（get lost）回不了旅馆。于是，他在＿＿＿＿旅馆的第一个路口停下来，拿出笔记本，＿＿＿＿＿记下了那家旅馆所在街道的街名，然后放心地走了。后来他＿＿＿＿迷路了，他在街上转了好几小时，才找到一个派出所（police station）。＿＿＿＿语言不通，警察搞不明白他的意思。于是他把记着街道＿＿＿＿＿的笔记本给警察看，可是警察还是不明白。后来警察请来了一位翻译，这位老外对翻译说："＿＿＿＿我不知道旅馆的名称，但是我知道旅馆＿＿＿＿＿街道的名称。"说着，他把笔记本交给翻译。翻译一看，纸上＿＿＿＿：单行道。

CHINESE IN STEPS 4   Lesson 40

认字识词 Words with Known Characters

1. 查找出下列词语的词义，并翻译成英文。

博士 _____	帝国 _____
教堂 _____	模式 _____
米色 _____	如何 _____
主人 _____	主任 _____
微观 _____	出口 _____

2. 翻译下列词语，并找出其结构规律。请至少再找出五个同样结构的词。

中行 _____	港商 _____
北师大 _____	女友 _____
高校 _____	人大 _____
交警 _____	亚运会 _____
影星 _____	上合组织 _____
名医 _____	数理化 _____

翻译练习 Translation

Say the following sentences in Chinese first and then write them out in characters.

1) The doctor does not allow you to eat anything before your medical check-up today.
2) The premier is going to hold a welcome banquet for him in the Great Hall of the People today.
3) Things are very expensive in that country. You won't be able to go for a holiday without taking a few thousand US dollars.
4) This group of buildings are about 5000 square kilometres.
5) Do you know the name of the last emperor in China?
6) Though what he said was not entirely true, nevertheless I don't think he meant to cheat you.

阅读 Reading

成语故事 The stories behind Chinese idioms

愚公移山 (yú gōng yí shān)

从前有一位老人，名叫愚公。他住在华北，他的家门面对着两座大山，这两座大山挡住(dǎng zhù)(blocked)了他家的出路。这两座山一座叫做太行山，一座叫做王屋山。愚公下决心率领(shuài lǐng)(led)他的儿子们把这两座大山搬走。有个名叫智叟(zhì sǒu)的老头看了发笑，说："你们这样干太愚蠢(yú chǔn)(stupid)了，你们父子数人要挖掉(wā diào)(move away)这样两座大山是完全不可能的。"愚公回答说："我死了以后有我的儿子，儿子死了又有孙子，子子孙孙是不会穷尽(end)的。这两座山虽然很高，可是不会再增(zēng)高(grow)了，挖一点就会少一点，有什么挖不平的呢？"愚公每天挖山不止。这件事感动(moved)了天帝，他就派了两个神仙(shén xiān)(immortal)下凡(come down to the world)，把这两座山背走了。

实用练习 Module Practice

写一篇文章，介绍一个城市。这个城市可以是北京，也可以是上海、南京等其他城市。文章越长越好。你要挑战自己，看看自己能写多长。

汉字笔顺 Stroke Order

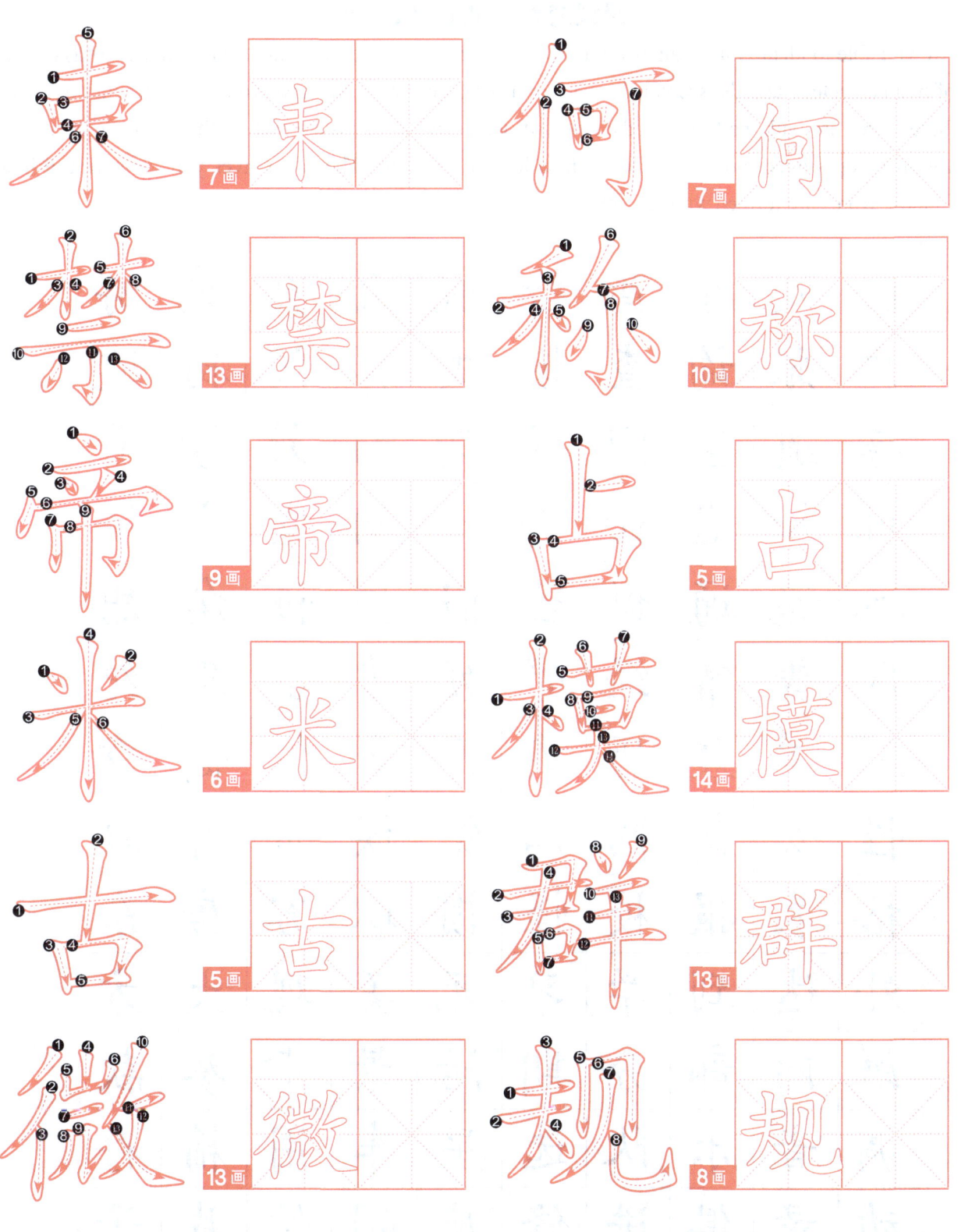

附录一 Appendix 1

组词游戏　Word Game

Are you able to identify a certain pattern of word formation in the following table? All the words consist of two-characters, and the second character of a word also starts the next word. Can you find out what these words are with the help of a dictionary if necessary, and translate each of them into English? Can you make up a list of your own and see how long it might be? The game gives you some idea of how Chinese words are formed with characters.

住	处	务	商	检	航	天	真	览	游
户	账	询	查	模	失	算	阅	街	逛
德	道	空	问	规	约	预	教	读	看
址	知	名	话	讲	定	购	堂	书	法
地	遍	通	说	理	假	型	证	念	想
区	普	常	经	管	发	准	备	思	纪
别	单	装	历	染	开	会	体	健	意
性	女	简	阴	阳	错	误	员	身	康
格	表	报	校	怪	惯	职	客	房	东
外	达	到	学	习	死	美	观	大	方
语	内	部	分	期	活	景	卡	参	款
调	音	乐	队	选	星	车	用	箱	存
动	录	俱	进	修	座	明	信	片	子
取	像	目	前	行	银	码	密	封	面

附录二　Appendix 2

听力原文　Listening Scripts

预备课

　　我昨天在出租车上把我的行李丢了。我拿了好多行李，很累。一路上司机总是跟我说话，问这问那。下车的时候，我只拿了车后备箱里的两个大箱子，忘了拿座位上的小箱子。小箱子里面有我每天都要用的东西，还有我给朋友从英国带来的生日礼物。我很生气，也很着急，可是不知道怎么办好。昨天一晚上都没睡好觉。没想到今天早上八点钟就有人来找我。我开门一看，是楼下看门的师傅，还有昨天的司机。他手里提着我的小箱子。原来司机发现了我的箱子，看到上面有我的行李卡，卡上有我的地址，就把箱子给我送来了。我当时要给他一百块钱，谢谢他，可是他就是不收。我就请他到一家大饭店吃了一顿西餐。明天有时间我一定写封信给出租车公司老板，谢谢这位好司机。

问题
1. 她在哪里把行李丢了？
2. 她怎么把行李丢了？
3. 行李里面有什么？
4. 发现行李丢了以后，她做了什么？
5. 今天早上谁来找她？
6. 司机从哪儿看到她的地址？
7. 她为什么请司机吃饭？
8. 她要给谁写信？

第三十一课

听力练习一

　　Jack 是英国 Scotland 人。他是 Glasgow 大学中文系的学生。他很喜欢中国文学。今年他到北京大学中文系学习。还没有开学，他就早早来到了北京。他游览了很多地方，也参观了北京图书馆。他说他现在更喜欢中国文化了。

　　今天是北京大学开学的第一天。他高高兴兴地去北京大学注册报到。可是到了注册站，他找不到录取通知书了。他马上跑回宿舍，找遍了他的房间，就是找不到他的录取通知书。最后他想起来了，昨天他带了录取通知书去地铁站买月票，回来以后把通知书和月票都放在书包里了。可是书包在哪儿呢？啊，想起来了！书包让他的朋友王英拿走了！

问题

1. Jack 是哪国人？
2. 开学前他做什么了？
3. 开学的那天他在找什么？
4. 为什么没有找到？

听力练习二

职员：下一位！

Jack：您好。我，我……

职员：你的护照和录取通知书呢？

Jack：这是我的护照，可是我的通知书……

职员：丢了？

Jack：我放在包里，可是包被我的朋友拿走了。

职员：那你打电话让他送来。

Jack：他现在不在北京，所以……真对不起。您能不能帮帮我？

职员：你是哪个系的？学什么专业？

Jack：我是中文系的。我学中国现代文学。

职员：你是读学位还是进修的？

Jack：我是读学位的。

职员：好，我查一下电脑……找到了。我给你系里打个电话，你等一会儿。

Jack：谢谢。

职员：行了！请你到那边去交费。

Jack：谢谢你了。再见。

职员：不谢，再见！

问题

5. 注册老师向 Jack 要录取通知书和什么？
6. Jack 要到哪个系学习？
7. 发现 Jack 没带录取通知书，注册老师做了什么？
8. 最后注册老师让 Jack 去哪儿了？

第三十二课

听力练习一

马里：美女，你真漂亮，我能请你跳舞吗？

小云：谢谢，你很会说话。

马里：是吗？你叫什么名字？

小云：我叫张小云。你呢？
马里：我叫马里。你的舞跳得很好。你一定常常参加舞会吧？
小云：也不常参加。我爸爸、妈妈不让。
马里：你爸爸妈妈一定是老师吧？
小云：你怎么知道？他们都是教书的。
马里：他们教什么呢？
小云：我爸爸在北大教数学，我妈妈在音乐学院教音乐。
马里：真巧！我是音乐学院的学生，今天才刚注册。你妈贵姓？
小云：我妈姓方，可是她这学期上不了班了。
马里：那为什么？
小云：我妈妈开车出事了，上星期才刚刚出院。
马里：我能去看看她吗？
小云：当然可以。你什么时候来我家？
马里：明天晚上，行吗？
小云：行。

问题
1. 小云和马里是在哪儿认识的？
2. 小云的爸爸妈妈是做什么工作的？
3. 马里学什么专业？
4. 小云的妈妈为什么这学期不教课？
5. 马里什么时候去看小云的妈妈？

听力练习二

中国人和美国人一样，都很喜欢打篮球。在中国差不多每个大学、中学、小学都有篮球场地。下午下课以后，同学们都喜欢去打一场篮球。中国有一个年轻人篮球打得很好。他是上海人，他出生于1980年9月12日，身高2米26，体重125公斤。他妈妈以前也是个很有名的篮球运动员。这个人就是姚明。现在他在美国打球。你知道姚明的球衣是多少号吗？是西方人不喜欢的13号。

问题
6. 下课以后，中国学生喜欢做什么？
7. 中国最有名的篮球运动员叫什么名字？
8. 他妈妈以前做什么工作？
9. 他的身高是多少？
10. 他的球衣是多少号？

第三十三课

听力练习一

　　Jack 来到北京以后，就到北京王府井的中国银行开了一个账户。他把带来的旅行支票存进了银行的账户里。可是他还没有信用卡，也没有拿到提款卡。今天他想去取点儿钱。他来到了银行，银行里人很多。这要等多长时间啊？他只好站在那里等。他一边排队，一边看书。一个服务员走过来问他："先生，你也取款吗？"他说是的。那个服务员告诉他，他应该去另一边排队。他跟着那个服务员来到了另一个窗口，那里一个人也没有。原来这是专给美元账户的人开的窗口。

　　问题

1. Jack 在哪儿开的账户？
2. 他是怎么把外汇带进中国的？
3. 看到银行里人很多，Jack 做了什么？
4. 为什么他能到另一个窗口取钱？

听力练习二

　　职员：您好，先生。

　　Jack：您好，我想取三千美元。

　　职员：请您下个星期来取。我们支行不保存美元，要到总行去取。所以你得提前一个星期通知我们。

　　Jack：那我不取美元了，我要人民币。我要兑换三千美元的人民币。

　　职员：那可以。请您填一张取款单，您带证件了吗？

　　Jack：带了，这是我的护照。

　　职员：好，请输入你的密码。

　　Jack：好。这样行了吧？

　　职员：您的密码不对。请您再试一下。

　　Jack：什么，怎么会不对呢？我再试试。

　　职员：还是不对。

　　Jack：我能再试一下吗？

　　职员：可以。对不起，您的密码还是不对。

　　Jack：我真的忘了，怎么办呢？

　　职员：您得再申请一个新的密码。请您填张表，签上名字，下个星期来取。

　　Jack：好。那我今天可以取钱吗？

　　职员：对不起，你今天取不了，下个星期再来取吧。

　　问题

5. Jack 原来打算取什么钱？

6. 后来为什么不取了？
7. Jack 第一次填的是什么表？
8. 他为什么没有换到人民币？

第三十四课

听力练习一

　　Mary 来到北京以后，买了不少明信片和手工艺品。那些明信片和手工艺品是送给她同学的。她还买了两套奥运会纪念品，奥运会就是 Olympic 运动会的意思。每套纪念品都有五个特别漂亮的小娃娃，他们的名字是：贝贝，晶晶，欢欢，迎迎，妮妮，连起来就是"北京欢迎你"。来中国以前，Mary 在英国电视台上看见过，Mary 的妹妹一定要 Mary 买一套送给她，还叫 Mary 一到北京就买。她到北京以后，找了好几家商店才发现了两套。她买下了那两套。她自己要留下一套。中国的旗袍也很漂亮，Mary 给妈妈买了一件。爸爸喜欢中国画儿，她给爸爸买了一幅中国画儿。爷爷奶奶都喜欢绣花睡衣，她给他们一人买了一件。东西买了不少，可是怎么寄回去呢？今天她没有课，想到邮局去问问怎么寄好。

　　问题
　　1. Mary 给她同学买了什么？
　　2. 五个奥运娃娃的名字连起来是什么？
　　3. 她为什么买了两套娃娃？
　　4. 她给妈妈买了什么？
　　5. 她给爷爷买了什么？

听力练习二

　　Mary：请问这儿可以寄包裹吗？
　　职员：当然可以。你寄什么？
　　Mary：我寄手工艺品和衣服。
　　职员：你先买一只箱子，把你要寄的东西放进去。然后填一张表。
　　Mary：这样行了吗？
　　职员：你还要把包裹打开，让我检查一下。
　　Mary：好，请你检查。
　　职员：这瓶子里是什么？
　　Mary：啊，我忘了告诉你了。这是药，是红花油，我爸爸常常背痛，他要我寄一瓶给他。
　　职员：那你得另外打一个包裹，不能和这些东西一起寄。
　　Mary：好。我把红花油拿出来。
　　职员：你要空运还是海运？

Mary：海运吧，海运便宜一些，他们不等着用。
职员：好，请支付750块人民币。把箱子交给我就行了。
Mary：好，谢谢，再见。

问题
6. Mary 要先买一个什么？
7. 瓶子里面是什么东西？
8. 她爸爸有什么病？
9. 她为什么要海运？
10. Mary 要支付多少钱？

第三十五课

听力练习一

小王：小李，今天你怎么这么漂亮？头发都变了样。
小李：别提了！今天我气死了。
小王：为什么？
小李：我到市中心的理发店理发，那个理发师把我的头发剪得这么短，还把我的头发染成这个怪样子……
小王：你有没有搞错？如果你不同意，他能帮你剪吗？
小李：我同意她剪，也同意她染，可我没有叫她把我的头发剪成这样，染成这样。
小王：到底怎么回事？你能不能说清楚一点儿？
小李：是这样的。我一进理发店那个理发师就给我洗头。她一边洗，一边说，现在很流行剪短发，说我长得漂亮，剪成短发，一定和电影明星一样。
小王：那你就同意了？
小李：我就同意了。她就拿起剪子来剪，一剪子下去，我就知道剪得太短了。我说剪得太短了。她说："你为什么不早说哪？现在剪下来了，接不上去了。"
小王：她说得对，那就是你的不是了。
小李：连你也这么说？！

问题
1. 小王为什么说小李今天很漂亮？
2. 小李为什么很生气？
3. 小李为什么同意理发师把头发剪短？
4. 小王说是谁的错？

听力练习二

小李：后来我只好让她剪了，她就把我剪成现在这个样子。

小王：还可以，不算难看。

小李：剪好了，那里的理发师都说，帅极了。他们还说，这种发型加上点红颜色才棒呢。

小王：你又同意了？

小李：我还没说"同意"，她已经给我染上了。

小王：原来你没有同意啊？！那你为什么不能去找她的经理？

小李：找她经理干什么？

小王：告她，告她对顾客服务不好。

小李：不行啊。

小王：那为什么？她就是经理吗？

小李：不是，她是我男朋友的妹妹。

小王：原来是这样！

问题

5. 小李的头发染成了什么颜色？
6. 谁说加上这种颜色才棒？
7. 为什么小李不去找经理？
8. 那个理发师是谁？

第三十六课

听力练习一

我叫王为。我每天一大早就起来读汉语。因为我的妈妈是中国人，她要我学习中国文化，她把中国的文化都一一介绍给我和我的妹妹。她还要我们学习中国人，早睡早起，所以我每天早上六点半就起床。我同宿舍的同学马修和我不一样，他睡得很晚，起得也很晚。等我读完书，吃好早饭，已经是九点了。这时候马修才起床。他没有时间吃早饭，天天如此。

今天我们有写作课。我读完书，吃完早饭，正准备去学校，看到我的朋友还在床上，我就对他说："马修，快起来，九点多了，你要迟到了！"可是马修说："今天十点有一场足球赛，我不想去上课了。你给我请一个假吧，就说我身体不舒服，怎么样？"我心里不同意，可是还是说"好。"

问题

1. 王为为什么早睡早起？
2. 他起床后通常做什么？
3. 马修通常几点起床？
4. 马修为什么今天要请假？

听力练习二

老师：同学们早！

学生们：老师早！

老师：今天为什么那么多同学没有来？

学生：老师，李健病了。她昨天在街上吃了一些北京小吃，今天早上拉肚子了。我送她去医院，她住院了。她要我替她请假。

老师：天气热，吃东西要小心。我下课以后去医院看她。大卫为什么没来？

学生：他说他病了，感冒了，今天不能来上课。他说他向你请假了。

老师：我想起来了，他昨晚给我发了个短信。马修也感冒了吗？王为，你和他一个宿舍，你一定知道。

王为：老师，他要我请假，他说他不舒服。

老师：不舒服？我现在给他打个电话。我可以用一下你的手机吗？

王为：可以。

马修：（接电话）喂，小王，比赛棒极了。现在是一比一。哎，你帮我请假了没有？

老师：马修，是我，张老师。我听说你病了，我借王为的手机给你打电话。

马修：张老师，真不好意思，我没病，我想看这场球赛……

老师：原来如此！这样很不好，你应该讲实话。

马修：对不起，老师。我以后再也不这样了。我现在马上就来上课。

问题

5. 李健为什么没来上课？
6. 李健现在在哪儿？
7. 大卫为什么没来上课？
8. 老师怎么知道了马修没来的原因？

第三十七课

听力练习一

大明来到中国以后，游览了很多地方。他深深地爱上了中国的一切。前几天，他到山东旅游，住在一位大妈家里。他写信把这件事告诉爸爸妈妈了。大明的爸爸妈妈是中文老师，所以他用中文给爸爸妈妈写信。没想到妈妈接到信以后马上来中国找他了。这到底是为什么呢？妈妈见到他以后赶紧问他："你还好吗？"他说："我没有病呀？！"妈妈说："身体没病，脑子是不是出了毛病？"大明说："怎么会呢？我很正常。""那你为什么和马一起住，一起吃草呢？"妈妈问他。原来大明写错字了。他把大妈写成了"大马"，把菜写成"草"了。他告诉爸爸妈妈，他跟大马住在一起，每天跟大马一起到地里干活，一起吃新鲜草。这可把爸爸妈妈急坏了。

问题
1. 大明的爸爸妈妈做什么工作？
2. 大明前几天在哪儿旅游？
3. 为什么妈妈去中国找他？
4. 大明想写哪两个字？

听力练习二

邮递员：您早！
大　明：您早！有我的信吗？
邮递员：信倒是没有，有一张明信片。
大　明：明信片？谁寄给我的？
邮递员：你自己看看。
大　明：啊，是从上海寄的，一定是我的朋友王京寄的。
邮递员：你再仔细看看。
大　明：啊，这不是我寄出去的明信片吗？怎么又回来了？
邮递员：是啊，怎么又回来了？
大　明：我没有把地址写错呀？！我特别注意把收信人的地址写在上面。
邮递员：对，地址没有写反。
大　明：那到底是为什么？
邮递员：你不觉得上面少了点儿什么吗？
大　明：什么也没少，我寄出的时候就这样。
邮递员：我是说明信片上面应该有的东西，而你的上面没有。
大　明：我真的看不出，请你告诉我吧。
邮递员：你没有贴邮票啊，先生！

问题
5. 大明收到了什么？
6. 是谁寄给他的？
7. 他信封上的地址是怎么写的？
8. 东西为什么又回来了？

第三十八课

听力练习一

马里来中国学习中文已经快一年了。最近，他想去找一个工作。他找工作的原因有两个：第一个，他要自食其力。什么是自食其力呢？自食其力就是自己靠自己生活，不要爸爸妈妈的钱。他说："虽然我爸爸很有钱，他不要我去打工，可是我已经二十一岁了，我可以靠自己的两只手生存。"第二个原因是他想通过打工提高中文水平。他有很多英国朋友，英国朋友看到他，都喜欢跟他讲英语。他也有很多中国朋友，可是他们都想跟他练习英语，从来不跟他说汉语。他跟他们说过好几次，要他们说汉语，可是没有用，他们还是说英语。他也就不好意思再要求他们了。他想，只有去打工练汉语了。他写信申请了几个单位。可是连一个面试的机会都没有。最近，他到一家合资公司去申请工作。他参加了面试。一开始，老板很高兴，说："你的汉语讲得很不错。"可是，当他拿出他的简历时，老板改变了主意，让他回家听信。他很难过。

问题
1. 马里来中国多久了？
2. 他为什么要去打工？
3. 他为什么不能跟他的中国朋友练习汉语？
4. 他为什么没有被合资公司录用？

听力练习二

马里：嗨，没想到在中国找工作也这么难！
朋友：听你的口气，在英国找工作一定也不容易了。
马里：是啊，在英国找工作也不容易。一个工作，几十个人申请。
朋友：在中国是一个工作，几百个人申请。
马里：真的？普通的工作也是这样吗？
朋友：是啊，工资比较高的更是不得了。
马里：中国好像失业的人不多，大家都在工作。
朋友：没办法，总得吃饭啊！
马里：大学生找工作难不难？
朋友：说难也难，说不难也不难。有的人高不成低不就，所以很难找到工作。
马里：什么是高不成低不就？
朋友：就是差的工作他不想去；好的工作呢，人家不要他。
马里：哦。可是我不是高不成低不就，怎么我还是找不到工作呢？
朋友：简历也很重要。简历写得好，往往成功了一半。
马里：我的工作经历不多，写来写去写不出东西来。
朋友：那你把求职信好好写一下。把你的爱好、能力都写出来。
马里：你帮我把求职信改一改，好不好？
朋友：没问题。我一定会把你推销出去。

问题
5. 在英国，一个工作一般有多少人申请？
6. 在中国，一个工作一般有多少人申请？

7. 为什么有的大学生找不到工作?
8. 马里的朋友要帮助他修改什么?

第三十九课

听力练习一

春节快到了！春节是中国人最大、最重要的节日。今年的春节是王力大学毕业以后的第一个春节。他上个月才找到了一个他喜欢的工作。现在的工资是一个月三千元。不仅如此，他还找到了一个漂亮的女朋友。因为他一个人在这个城市工作，他的女朋友请他去她家过年。这真是喜上加喜，他高兴极了。今天是星期天，一大早，他的女朋友就来找他一起去南京路买东西。南京路上人来人往，每家店里都是人山人海。他问他的女朋友："你爸爸、妈妈喜欢什么东西？"他女朋友说："不管是什么东西，只要是我们买的，他们都会喜欢的。"她还说："爸爸妈妈知道你刚开始工作，没有多少钱，有个礼物意思意思就行了。"可是王力说："第一次见面，一定要送个贵重的礼物，礼物轻了就是对老人不尊重。"正说着，他看到了一件适合老人的礼物，他马上要买，可是他的钱包不见了……

问题
1. 王力每月的工资是多少?
2. 为什么说王力这个春节喜上加喜?
3. 他们去南京路给谁买礼物?
4. 他为什么没有买?

听力练习二

王力：　嗨，我的钱包不见了。
女朋友：真的？你是不是忘带了？
王力：　肯定带了，我出门的时候检查过了。
女朋友：刚才我看到有个十几岁的孩子在我们身边。会不会是他偷的？
王力：　哪一个小孩？
女朋友：就是那一个！
王力：　喂，你，你刚才是不是偷了我的钱包？
女朋友：我看到你一直在我们的身边。
小孩：　放开我，你们在说什么呀？
王力：　你偷了我的钱包。
小孩：　我没有偷什么钱包，我从来不偷东西！
女朋友：你把钱包交出来吧，不然我们要报警了。
小孩：　你的钱包是什么样的？你认得出你的钱包吗？
王力：　当然认得出！瞧，警察来了。警察，我们抓到了一个小偷！

女朋友： 他偷了我们的钱包，我们把他抓住了。
警察： 等一等，你是说你的钱包不见了？
王力： 是的，我的钱包不见了。刚才他就在我们旁边。
警察： 这孩子不是小偷。他看到一个小偷就报告了我们。我们把小偷抓住了。这个小偷偷了好几个钱包，你们看看，哪个是你们的？
王力： 这个是。钱也没有少。对不起，我们错怪了这孩子。
女朋友： 对不起，真不好意思。谢谢你。
小孩： 不谢，再见。警察叔叔再见。

问题
5. 王力什么时候检查了钱包？
6. 为什么他们以为是那个孩子偷了钱？
7. 警察为什么不抓那个孩子？
8. 那个小孩做了什么好事？

第四十课

听力练习一

王京是个足球运动员，他的身体很棒。他常常到世界各地旅游，爬山是他最喜爱的运动。今年他有机会到中国参加足球比赛。他高兴极了，因为他一直都想来中国。这次，他比其他队员提前两天到了北京。到北京后，一放下行李他就急忙去参观天安门和故宫。第二天，他就上了长城。他早就知道毛主席说过"不到长城非好汉"，所以他一定要当上好汉。他站在长城上，照了好几张相。他把相片寄回家，还打电话告诉他爸爸妈妈说："现在我登上了长城，可以算一个好汉了！"他爸爸妈妈听了非常高兴，说："我们明年夏天一定也来当一次好汉。"

问题
1. 王京最喜欢做什么？
2. 他来中国做什么？
3. 下面这些地点，王京哪个没去过？
4. 王京的爸爸妈妈明年来中国干什么？

听力练习二

爸爸： 谢谢你，王京。这些日子你给我们当向导，真是帮了我们的大忙。
王京： 哪儿的话，儿子为父母做事是应该的。
妈妈： 没想到我儿子懂事多了。给爸爸妈妈做事不要钱了。
王京： 我从中国这儿学到了不少东西。对不起，妈，我以前不该要你们的钱。
爸爸： 没什么，不同的地方有不同的文化。你在英国干活拿钱是应该的。

妈妈：我倒是喜欢中国文化，你帮我，我帮你，不要太计较。
王京：可是中国正在改变，有些年轻人觉得西方的观念好，也开始计较了。
妈妈：我注意到了。服务员很在意小费。
爸爸：人家给你服务，给人家小费是应该的。
妈妈：王京，要陪我们去西安的那位姑娘，你看我们应该给她多少小费？
王京：妈，你不用管了，我来处理就行了。
爸爸：虽然是你的好朋友，可是我们也不能白用人家。
王京：爸，你就别管了。她很想认识你们。
爸爸：想认识我们？她是不是在追你？
妈妈：谁追谁还说不定呢！
王京：你们搞错了，她只是我的一个普通朋友，她是我同班同学李明的妹妹。

问题

5. 为什么妈妈说王京懂事了？
6. 王京从中国学到了什么？
7. 王京的爸爸妈妈明天要去哪儿？
8. 谁陪他们去？

附录三　Appendix 3

练习答案 Keys to the Exercises

预备课

听力练习

1) a　　2) c　　3) c　　4) a　　5) b　　6) c　　7) c　　8) b

语法练习

1. 多项选择

1) b　　2) c　　3) c　　4) a　　5) b　　6) c　　7) b　　8) a
9) c　　10) a

2. 选词填空

着、着、正、着、正、正、得、到、就、得、了、过

认字识词

1.

名词	noun	动词	verb
形容词	adjective	副词	adverb
代词	pronoun	专有名词	proper noun
数词	numeral	量词	measure word
介词	preposition	连词	conjunction
感叹词	exclamatory word	象声词	onomatopoeia

翻译练习

1) 我能把行李放（在）这儿吗？

2) 书太多了，我的包装不下。

3) 去德比的票多少钱一张？

4) 你能帮我先付上酒钱吗？

5) 交通是这儿最大的问题。

6) 上海的天气和伦敦的差不多。

7) 你的行李太重了，拿不上飞机。

8) 我十二月总是很忙，连去看我妈妈的时间都没有。

9) 我没想到他已经六十多岁了，因为他看起来只有四十几 / 多岁。

10) 对不起，我得先看看你的护照才可以给你票。

第三十一课

听力练习

1) c   2) a   3) b   4) c   5) b   6) a   7) b   8) c

多项选择

1) b   2) c   3) a   4) a   5) c   6) b   7) a   8) c

选词填空

读、考试、一起、如果、可以、报到、和、然后、大约、参加

认字识词

1.
总数	total amount	注意	pay attention to/attention
画册	pictorial	杂物	miscellaneous goods
思想	thinking/ideology	游览	tour/sightseeing
阅读	reading	比如	for instance
修理	repair	学科	subject of study

2.
老汉	old man	老虎	tiger
老公	husband	老婆	wife
老大	eldest	老小	youngest
小吃	snack	小费	tip
小店	little shop	小菜	side dish
小人书	picture story book	小朋友	children

翻译练习

1) 大英图书馆的阅览室没有空调。
2) 我们明天十二点在我办公室对面的咖啡馆见面，好吗？
3) 我找不到你的名字。你预订房间了吗？
4) 要学习中文/汉语的同学请到二楼注册。
5) 我是从越南来的，他是从马里来的。
6) 你得先付房钱，不然我不能给你钥匙。

第三十二课

听力练习

1) c   2) c   3) a   4) a   5) b   6) c   7) a   8) c
9) c   10) b

多项选择

1) b   2) c   3) a   4) b   5) a   6) c   7) a   8) b

选词填空

那儿、种、滑草、感觉、蓝、绿、差不多、一开始、就像、人们

认字识词

1. 选美　　　　beauty pageant　　　干活　　　work
   私自　　　　secretively　　　　　自私　　　selfish
   武打　　　　kung fu fight　　　　目前　　　for the time being
   活鱼　　　　fresh/live fish　　　死人　　　deceased person
   队长　　　　team captain　　　　证人　　　witness
2. 房子　　　　house　　　　　　　 演员　　　actor/actress
   脑子　　　　brain　　　　　　　　卫生员　 assistant nurse, first-aider
   篮子　　　　basket　　　　　　　警卫员　 guard
   读者　　　　reader　　　　　　　科学家　 scientist
   记者　　　　journalist　　　　　歌唱家　 singer
   作者　　　　writer　　　　　　　数学家　 mathematician

翻译练习

1) 他昨天又迟到了，可是他好像一点儿也不觉得不好意思。
2) 我女朋现在不仅每天去健身房，而且还请了一个私人教练。
3) 乒乓球在中国很流行，大部分大学都有球队。
4) 他不是不想吃，而是病了吃不下。
5) 中国书法很漂亮，可是看起来很难学。你觉得我学得会吗？
6) 我们什么时候可以注册功夫课？我从小就对这很感兴趣。

第三十三课

听力练习
1) a　　2) c　　3) c　　4) b　　5) b　　6) a　　7) a　　8) b

多项选择
1) c　　2) b　　3) a　　4) a　　5) b　　6) a　　7) c　　8) b

选词填空
了、过、多少、当时、最高的、站着、先进、进口

认字识词

1. 管理　　　　manage　　　　　　　　　　　管家　　　housekeeper
   账本　　　　(account) book　　　　　　　 算账　　　settle account
   奖金　　　　bonus　　　　　　　　　　　　丢面子　 lose face
   提货单　　　bill of landing/delivery order　寄存处　(luggage) deposit
   香水　　　　perfume　　　　　　　　　　　香米　　　fragrant rice
2. 道路　　　　road　　　　　　　　　　　　喜爱　　　love
   数量　　　　amount　　　　　　　　　　　变化　　　change

歌唱	sing	城市	city
光亮	light	生产	produce
表格	form	等候	wait
偷盗	steal	存放	deposit, leave with

翻译练习

1) 不管他去不去，我们明天都要去。
2) 谢天谢地，我的钱包没丢。我差点把我的信用卡停了。
3) 现在信用卡都要有个人密码。
4) 如果你想申请这个工作，你得填张表寄给那个公司。
5) 香港人很多，房子一般很高，但是房间都比较小。
6) 用自动取款机取钱很方便。你什么时候取都行。

第三十四课

听力练习

1) c　　2) b　　3) c　　4) a　　5) a　　6) c　　7) b　　8) a
9) b　　10) a

多项选择

1) a　　2) c　　3) a　　4) c　　5) b　　6) a　　7) b　　8) a

选词填空

一般、又、使用、中间、到、小月、如、只有

认字识词

1.
邮递员	postman	顺利	smoothly
念书	study/read	车轮	wheel
太阳	sun	办事处	office
阳光	sunshine	月光	Moonlight
邮电局	post office	警察局	police station

2.
始终	from beginning to end	长短	length
阴阳	Yin and Yang	是非	right and wrong
老少	old and young	冷热	cold and hot; temperature
真假	true and false	死活	life or death; anyway
来往	contact	文武	civil and military
早晚	sooner or later	轻重	weight

翻译练习

1) 这个邮局是由中国邮政管理的。
2) 我想买一些北京的纪念邮票。

3) 我是1985年出生的，你知道我属什么吗？

4) 我原来（是）吃肉（的）。后来医生告诉我最好多吃蔬菜和水果。从那以后，我就再也不吃肉了 / 我就再也没吃过肉。

5) 为什么我上月在中国寄的包裹还没有到？

6) 你的包裹是怎么寄的？海运还是空运？

第三十五课

听力练习

1) b   2) c   3) a   4) b   5) c   6) b   7) c   8) a

多项选择

1) b   2) a   3) b   4) c   5) c   6) b   7) a   8) c

选词填空

让、以外、顾客、只能、只好、还是、虽然、起来、可以、而是

认字识词

1. 护士　　nurse　　　　　　　　平常　　usually
   明显　　obvious　　　　　　　总之　　in short
   洗钱　　money laundering　　　洗礼　　baptize
   照顾　　take care of　　　　　宾馆　　hotel
   染色体　chromosome　　　　　　井井有条　in perfect order
2. 黑豆　　black bean　　　　　　明文　　proclaimed in writing
   红牌　　red card　　　　　　　黄牌　　yellow card
   美酒　　fine wine　　　　　　　香菜　　coriander
   怪话　　cynical remarks　　　　短路　　short circuit
   平地　　flat land　　　　　　　冷盘　　cold dish
   空位　　empty seat　　　　　　旧车　　old car

翻译练习

1) 我喜欢短头发，洗起来很容易 / 很容易洗。

2) 那儿烫发和染发都很便宜。连烫带染不到80英镑。

3) 他看起来有点生气了。我知道他已经一个多月没有休息了。

4) 伦敦位于英国的东南部，离海不远。

5) 王先生是位出色的理发师，理发理得好极了。

6) 排队的人很多，要几个小时才能轮到你。

第三十六课

听力练习

1) c 2) a 3) b 4) b 5) a 6) a 7) c 8) b

多项选择

1) c 2) b 3) a 4) b 5) b 6) a 7) c 8) a

选词填空

关于、本来、范围、以为、出去、正式、容易、只好、不管、非常

认字识词

1. 办法　　　　method　　　　　　　同事　　　colleague
   内科　　　　internal medicine　　外科　　　surgery
   拉面　　　　hand-pulled noodles　地区　　　region
   签证　　　　visa　　　　　　　　　笨蛋　　　fool
   笨头笨脑　　blunder head　　　　　笨手笨脚　clumsy
2. 倒茶　　　　pour tea　　　　　　　洗车　　　wash car
   经商　　　　do business　　　　　扫地　　　sweep floor
   越级　　　　bypass the line manager　种菜　　grow/plant vegetables
   打字　　　　typing　　　　　　　　放羊　　　herd sheep
   拍电影　　　filming　　　　　　　　生孩子　　give birth to a child
   放火　　　　set fire　　　　　　　讲话　　　speaking

翻译练习

1) 我有点不舒服。你能替我写个病假条吗？
2) 我们谁也／都没想到他不会说汉语。
3) 我的手机没电了，没想到你的也没电了。我们怎么找人来帮助我们呢？
4) 就人口而言，中国是全球人口最多的国家。
5) 小王今天为什么穿得这么正式？
   谁知道呢！他最近一直很怪。
6) 我夏天去了新疆，那儿的烤羊肉真好吃／真香。

第三十七课

听力练习

1) b 2) a 3) a 4) c 5.b 6) a 7) c 8) b

多项选择

1) c 2) c 3) b 4) c 5) a 6) c 7) b 8) a

选词填空

时候、到、问、别人、后来、怎么、还是、吹、一点儿、就是

认字识词

1.
退休	retire	反对	against, oppose
误会	mistake	反义词	antonym
错误	error	同义词	synonym
靠近	come near	同音词	homophone
附件	attachment	老伴儿	old spouse

2.
干洗	dry clean	慢跑	jogging
高考	university entrance exam	大选	general election
巧遇	bump into sb.	冷烫	cold perm (hair)
单打	play singles	双打	play doubles
早婚	early marriage	晚婚	late marriage
紧靠	close by, next to	白吃	freeload

翻译练习

1) 昨天我在老王家的时候，看见他爷爷穿袍子留辫子的照片。
2) 今天早上路上没有公共汽车，你知道是怎么回事吗？
3) 一开始我不太懂那儿的人（说话）的口音，现在我已经习惯了。
4) 你说什么？他今天早上难道不是靠左边开车去上班的吗？
5) 这是一个多元的世界，在有些国家里，一个男人可以有好几个太太。
6) 我在南非居住了五年，在那里，我也交了很多朋友。

第三十八课

听力练习

1) a　　2) c　　3) b　　4) c　　5) b　　6) c　　7) c　　8) a

多项选择

1) a　　2) a　　3) b　　4) b　　5) b　　6) c　　7) b　　8) c

选词填空

招聘、精通、没想到、居然、广告、马上、使用、熟练、种、看着

认字识词

1.
西瓜	watermelon	建造	build
兰花	orchid	大众	mass, popular
事实	fact	高科技	high tech
传球	pass the ball	资本	(financial) capital
皇上	emperor	胜利	victory

2.
中国造	made in China	心算	mental calculation
口吃	stammer	自助	self-service

自主	independence	师传	pass on by master
手写	hand written	友爱	friendly affection
云游	roam	日出	sunrise
笔录	notes	鱼死网破	a life-and-death struggle

翻译练习

1) 我没想到他这么喜欢吹牛。
2) 我听说你们公司在招聘实习生，我对此很感/有兴趣。
3) 我们老师很有才华，她画儿画得很好。
4) 我去年去/访问了中国很多地方。中国人都非常热情。
5) 你有什么爱好/你的爱好是什么？我喜欢爬山、骑马、跳舞和看书。
6) 我有很多银行工作经验。我相信我能胜任这个工作。

第三十九课

听力练习

1) a　　2) c　　3) a　　4) b　　5) c　　6) b　　7) a　　8) b

多项选择

1) a　　2) c　　3) a　　4) a　　5) b　　6) c　　7) a　　8) b

选词填空

快、也、过、每年、一、没有、可是、不必、还是、与其

认字识词

1.
故事	story	陪同	accompany
理由	reason	骗子	cheater
鞋刷	shoe brush	廉价	cheap
随和	easy-going	购买	purchase
随身听	walkman	药膏	ointment

2.
改变	change	说明	explain
放大	amplify	完成	accomplish
识破	seen through	拉平	flatten out
表明	show	推进	push on
刷新	break the record/renovate	洗净	wash thoroughly
登高	climb	跌倒	fall down

翻译练习

1) 被他骗了几次以后，我们再也不（相）信他说的话了/他说什么我们都不信了。
2) 英国许多商店一月份都打折（卖它们的商品）。
3) 我父母/爸爸妈妈喜欢去自由市场买东西，因为那儿的东西物美价廉。

4) 下星期我们一定见（一）面。是我去你那儿还是你来我这儿？

5) 她故意买了这条大号连衣裙，因为她听说今年夏天流行这种款式／因为她听说这是今年夏天流行的款式。

6) 她是我们学校里最漂亮的姑娘，追她的帅哥多得不得了。

第四十课

听力练习

1) b   2) b   3) a   4) a   5) b   6) a   7) c   8) c

多项选择

1) b   2) c   3) a   4) b   5) c   6) a   7) c   8) a

选词填空

住下、因此、离开、仔细地、真的、由于、名称、虽然、所在、写着

认字识词

1. 博士　　　doctor (PhD)　　　帝国　　　empire
   教堂　　　church　　　　　　模式　　　mode
   米色　　　cream colour　　　如何　　　how
   主人　　　host　　　　　　　主任　　　director
   微观　　　micro　　　　　　 出口　　　exit
2. 中行　　　中国银行　　　　　港商　　　香港商人
   北师大　　北京师范大学　　　女友　　　女朋友
   高校　　　高等学校　　　　　人大　　　人民代表大会
   交警　　　交通警察　　　　　亚运会　　亚洲运动会
   影星　　　电影明星　　　　　上合组织　合作组织
   名医　　　有名的医生　　　　数理化　　数学、物理、化学

翻译练习

1) 今天体检／检查以前，医生禁止你吃任何东西。

2) 总理今天要为他在人民大会堂举行一个欢迎宴会。

3) 那个国家的东西很贵，没有几千美元你是不能去那儿度假的。

4) 这个建筑群大约占地5000平方公里。

5) 你知道中国末代／最后一个皇帝的名字吗？

6) 虽然他所说的不都是真的，但我想他不是故意骗你的。

附录四　Appendix 4

汉英词汇表　Chinese-English Vocabulary List

中文	拼音	词性	英文	课号
阿	ā	助	noun prefix	37
哎	āi	感叹	ah	36
爱好	àihào	名/动	hobby	38
阿拉伯	Ālābó	专名	Arab, Arabic	37
安	ān	名	peace	40
阿姨	āyí	名	aunt, term of address for a woman similar in age to one's parents	39
百货大楼	bǎihuòdàlóu	名	department store	39
办	bàn	动	do, handle	31
伴	bàn	名	companion	37
般	bān	助	type; like	31
棒	bàng	名/形	bat, stick; terrific (colloquial)	32
办公室	bàngōngshì	名	office	31
棒球	bàngqiú	名	baseball	32
办理	bànlǐ	动	deal with, process	31
宝	bǎo	名	treasure	39
保存	bǎocún	动	preserve	40
报到	bàodào	动	report one's arrival or presence	31
包裹	bāoguǒ	名	parcel	34
保险	bǎoxiǎn	形	safe	34
被	bèi	名	quilt	34
被套	bèitào	名	quilt cover	34
笨	bèn	形	stupid, slow	36
毕	bì	动	complete	38
辫	biàn	名	plaits	37
辫子	biànzi	名	plaits, pigtail	37
标	biāo	名/动	mark	33
表达	biǎodá	动/名	express; expression	37
表格	biǎogé	名	forms	31

标记	biāojì	名	mark	33
比较	bǐjiào	副/动	relatively; compare	33
宾	bīn	名	guest	35
比如	bǐrú	动	for example	34
必须	bìxū	情动	must	39
必要	bìyào	名/形	necessity; necessary	39
毕业	bìyè	动	graduate	38
伯	bó	名	uncle	37
博	bó	形	vast, extensive	40
博物馆	bówùguǎn	名	museum	40
部	bù	名	department, part, section	32
不管	bùguǎn	连	no matter	33
不好意思	bùhǎoyìsi	短语	embarrassed; sorry	32
不见得	bújiàndé	副	not necessarily	37
不仅	bùjǐn	连	not only	32
不仅……而且……	bùjǐn...érqiě		not only...but also...	32
不然	bùrán	连	otherwise, if not	31
不同	bùtóng	形	different	35
才	cái	名	talent	38
才华	cáihuá	名	talent	38
菜系	càixì	名	style of cooking, cuisine	31
参观	cānguān	动	visit and tour around (a place)	40
册	cè	名	volume, book	31
层	céng	量	floor; layer	36
长裙	chángqún	名	long skirt	39
抄	chāo	动	copy	36
超短裙	chāoduǎnqún	名	mini skirt	39
超市	chāoshì	名	supermarket	33
称	chēng	动	call; say	40
成为	chéngwéi	动	become	33
称为	chēngwéi	动	be called as	40
匙*	chí	名	spoon	31
迟	chí	形	late	32

迟到	chídào	动	arrive late	32
吃力	chīlì	形	strenuous, require great effort	37
处	chù	名	place; department	33
传	chuán	动	pass on	38
串	chuàn	名	bunch	36
床单	chuángdān	名	bed sheet	34
传真	chuánzhēn	名	fax	38
吹	chuī	动	blow dry	35
出色	chūsè	形	outstanding	35
出众	chūzhòng	形	outstanding	38
聪	cōng	形	clever	36
聪明	cōngming	形	intelligent, clever	36
从事	cóngshì	动	engaged in (for a job)	34
存	cún	动	deposit; store	33
错误	cuòwù	名	mistake, error	37
达	dá	动	reach	34
大部分	dàbùfen	名	most	32
大街	dàjiē	名	broadway; avenue	35
大量	dàliàng	副	a great quatity, a large number	31
单	dān	形/名	single; bill	33
单	dān	名	sheet	34
当场	dāngchǎng	副	on the spot, there and then	39
当年	dāngnián	名	at that time (year)	34
单裤	dānkù	名	unlined trousers; single layer of outer trousers	39
单位	dānwèi	名	unit	36
单元	dānyuán	名	unit; module	33
盗	dào	动	steal	33
到达	dàodá	动/名	arrive; arrivals	34
到底	dàodǐ	副	ultimately, in the end, after all	34
盗用	dàoyòng	动	embezzle	33
大型	dàxíng	形	large size	34
大约	dàyuē	副	approximately	31
打折	dǎzhé	动	give discount	39

递	dì	动	hand over	34
帝	dì	名	emperor, imperial	40
调	diào	名	intonation, tone	37
定期	dìngqī	名	fixed term	33
丢	diū	动	lose	33
地址	dìzhǐ	名	address	33
洞	dòng	名	hole	39
东单	Dōngdān	专名	a shopping street in Beijing	35
读	dú	动	read; study (a subject)	31
锻	duàn	动	forge	32
短	duǎn	形	short	35
锻炼	duànliàn	动	take physical exercise	32
队	duì	名	team	32
对内	duìnèi	介宾结构	internal	36
对外	duìwài	介宾结构	external	36
对外汉语	duìwài hànyǔ	名	Chinese as a foreign language	31
队员	duìyuán	名	team member	32
多元	duōyuán	形	diversified	37
多种多样	duōzhǒng duōyàng	形	various	33
而	ér		but	32
而且	érqiě	连	and; but also	32
发	fà	名	hair	35
范	fàn		limits	36
反	fǎn	形	opposite; against	37
访	fǎng	动	visit	40
方便	fāngbiàn	形	convenient	32
方法	fāngfǎ	名	method	36
方式	fāngshì	名	manner; approach	32
放心	fàngxīn	动	rest assure of	33
范围	fànwéi	名	scope, range	36
发型	fàxíng	名	hair style	35

肥	féi	形	fat	39
肥皂	féizào	名	soap	39
份	fèn	名	share	33
封	fēng	动/量	seal; m.w for letter	37
分行	fēnháng	名	branch	38
风险	fēngxiǎn	名	risk	38
附	fù	动	add, attach	37
副	fù	形	secondary; deputy, vice	38
府	fǔ	名	mansion	35
附上	fùshàng	动	attach	37
副修	fùxiū	动	minor in	38
改	gǎi	动	change, correct	32
改变	gǎibiàn	动	change	32
改造	gǎizào	动	transform	35
港	gǎng	名	harbour	33
港币	gǎngbì	专名	Hong Kong dollar	33
告	gào	动	tell	36
膏	gāo	名	paste	39
告诉	gàosù	动	tell	36
格	gé	名	square formed by cross lines; check	31
更改	gēnggǎi	动	change; alter	33
更加	gèngjiā	副	even more	36
格式	géshì	名	format	37
格外	géwài	副	especially, exceptionally	40
宫	gōng	名	palace	40
供	gōng	动	supply	35
公开	gōngkāi	动	publicize	36
工资	gōngzī	名	salary	38
购	gòu	动	purchase	39
狗不理包子	Gǒubùlǐbāozi	专名	a well known brand of steamed bun in Tianjin	37
购物	gòuwù	动+名	(go) shopping; shopping	39
狗熊	gǒuxióng	名	black bear; a coward	39
顾	gù	动	look after	35

故	gù	副/名/形	intentionally; cause; old	39
故	gù	形	old	40
古	gǔ	形	ancient	40
惯	guàn	动	spoil; be used to	37
管	guǎn	动	mind; manage	33
观	guān	动	look, observe	40
逛	guàng	动	walk around (shops), ramble, stroll	39
广场	guǎngchǎng	名	(city) square	32
广告	guǎnggào	名	advertisement	36
挂念	guàniàn	动	worry about; miss	37
管理	guǎnlǐ	动/名	manage; management	34
关于	guānyú	介	about	36
古代	gǔdài	名	ancient times	40
故宫	gùgōng	专名	The Forbidden City	40
规	guī	名/动	rule	40
贵宾	guìbīn	名	VIP	35
规模	guīmó	名	scale	40
建筑群	jiànzhùqún	名	cluster of buildings	40
顾客	gùkè	名	customer	35
裹	guǒ	名/动	wrap	34
锅	guō	名	pot	37
过冬	guòdōng	动	spend winter, go through winter	39
国际	guójì	名	international	33
故意	gùyì	副	intentionally	39
海德	Hǎidé	专名	Hyde (transliteration)	38
海运	hǎiyùn	名	transport by sea, surface mail	34
好	hào	动	like, love	37
好客	hàokè	形	be hospitable	37
好像	hǎoxiàng	副	seem, like	36
何	hé	名	which	40
华	huá	名	glamour	38
皇	huáng	名	emperor	38
皇帝	huángdì	名	emperor	40

皇宫	huánggōng	名	royal palace	40
皇家	huángjiā	名	royal family	38
惠	huì	动	benefit	39
会话	huìhuà	名	conversation	31
会员卡	huìyuán kǎ	名	membership card	32
活	huó	动/形	live; alive	32
货	huò	名	commodity, goods	33
或	huò	连	or	34
获	huò	动	capture, reap	37
伙	huǒ	名	mate	37
伙伴	huǒbàn	名	partner	37
货币	huòbì	名	currency	33
活动	huódòng	动/名	exercise; activity	32
火锅	huǒguō	名	hot pot	37
活期	huóqī	名	current (account)	33
或者	huòzhě	连	or	34
急	jí	形	pressing	34
际	jì	名	border, boundary	33
技	jì	名	skill	38
己	jǐ	代	oneself	36
价	jià	名	value, price	34
价格	jiàgé	名	price	34
健*	jiàn	形	healthy	31
建	jiàn	动	build	38
剪	jiǎn	动	cut	35
奖	jiǎng	名	reward	33
讲	jiǎng	动	talk	36
将	jiāng	副	will, about to, be going to	36
讲课	jiǎngkè	动	give lecture, teach	37
奖学金	jiǎngxuéjīn	名	scholarship	33
讲座	jiǎngzuò	名	lecture	36
健康	jiànkāng	形/名	healthy; health	37
健身	jiànshēn	名/动	keep fit	32

健身房	jiànshēnfáng	名	gym	32
建筑	jiànzhù	名	architecture, construction	38
较	jiào	副	compared with; comparably	33
交费	jiāofèi	动+名	pay fees	31
教练	jiàoliàn	名	coach, trainer	32
节	jié	量	period, session	32
界	jiè	名	circles; boundary	37
街	jiē	名	street	35
借记卡	jièjìkǎ	名	debit card	33
结束	jiéshù	动	finish, end	40
结算	jiésuàn	动	settle accounts	33
禁	jìn	动	forbid	40
仅	jǐn	副	only	32
紧	jǐn	形	tight	34
禁地	jìndì	名	forbidden place	40
技能	jìnéng	名	skill	38
敬	jìng		honour	36
井	jǐng	名	well	35
景	jǐng	名	scene	40
精	jīng	形	smart	35
精	jīng	形/名	perfect; accuracy	38
景点	jǐngdiǎn	名	tourist spot	40
京东	Jīngdōng	专名	Jingdong, Chinese online shopping website	39
敬礼	jìnglǐ	动	salute; yours sincerely(ending letter), extend greetings	36
经历	jīnglì	名/动	experience	38
精神	jīngshén	形/名	smart looking, lively	35
精通	jīngtōng	动/形	be proficient in	38
纪念	jìniàn	名/动	commemorate	34
纪念堂	jìniàntáng	名	memorial hall	40
紧急	jǐnjí	形	urgent, emergency	34
金融	jīnróng	名	finance	38
进行	jìnxíng	动	conduct, carry out	31
进修	jìnxiū	动	engage in advanced studies	31

禁止	jìnzhǐ	动	forbid	40
旧	jiù	形	old; used (not for age)	33
就业	jiùyè	动/名	get a job; employment	36
就座	jiùzuò	动	be seated, take one's seat	36
局	jú	名	bureau	34
俱	jù	形	all, complete	32
举	jǔ	动	hold up	40
居	jū	动	live	37
俱乐部	jùlèbù	名	club	32
居然	jūrán	副	unexpectedly	38
举行	jǔxíng	动	hold, take place	40
居住	jūzhù	名/动	habitation; live	37
卡	kǎ	名	card	32
开设	kāishè	动	set up, offer	31
开业	kāiyè	动	start/open (a business)	35
卡拉OK	kǎlā ok	名	karaoke	38
康	kāng	形	healthy	37
靠	kào	介/动	alongside; keep to; rely on	37
科	kē	名	branch; subject	31
空	kōng	名	sky; air	34
空调	kōngtiáo	名	air conditioner	31
空运	kōngyùn	名	transport by air, airmail	34
口头	kǒutóu	形	oral	36
夸	kuā	动	boast; praise	38
快递	kuàidì	名	express delivery	34
夸张	kuāzhāng	形/动	exaggerating; exaggerate	38
啦	la	助	a phrase-final particle (fusion of 了 + 啊)	37
拉	lā	动	pull; defecate	36
拉肚子	lādùzi	动	have diarrhoea	36
来访	láifǎng	动	come on a visit	40
来自	láizì	动	come from	31
兰	lán	名	orchid	38
览	lǎn	动	browse	31
老字号	lǎozìhào	名	long established brand (shop)	35

例	lì	名	instance	36
李健	Lǐ Jiàn	专名	a Chinese name	31
联	lián	动	connect	33
廉	lián	形	cheap	39
炼	liàn	动	refine	32
量	liàng	名	capacity; quantity	31
连剪带吹	liánjiǎndàichuī		cut and blow (hair)	35
连忙	liánmáng	副	hurriedly	39
联系	liánxì	动	contact	33
脸型	liǎnxíng	名	feature (of the face)	35
连衣裙	liányīqún	名	dress	39
聊	liáo	动	chat	32
聊天	liáotiān	动	chat	32
列	liè	名/动	rank	33
历法	lìfǎ	名	calendar	34
理发店	lǐfàdiàn	名	hairdressing salon	35
理发师	lǐfàshī	名	barber	35
理科	lǐkē	名	science (subjects of study)	31
力量	lìliàng	名	strength	31
另	lìng	形	other, another	33
零起点	língqǐdiǎn	名	ab initio; from scratch (starting from zero)	31
另外	lìngwài	副	besides, in addition	33
例外	lìwài	名	exception	37
利息	lìxi	名	interest (financial)	33
例子	lìzi	名	example	36
轮	lún	名	wheel	34
轮	lún	动/名	become one's turns; turn, wheel	35
轮船	lúnchuán	名	steamship	34
录取	lùqǔ	动/名	admission; admit (on a programme)	31
骂	mà	动	swear at, curse	39
马来西亚	Mǎláixīyà	专名	Malaysia	31
毛裤	máokù	名	long woollen underpants	39

毛主席	Máozhǔxí	专名	Chairman Mao	40
每	měi	代	every, each	31
美白美发厅	Měibái měifàtīng	专名	Meibai Hairdressing	35
美发	měifà	动+名	have one's hair styled	35
美国运通	Měiguó yùntōng	专名	American Express	33
美女	měinǚ	名	beautiful woman	39
美容	měiróng	动+名	cosmetology; improve one's looks	35
美容师	měiróng shī	名	beautician	35
门	mén	量	M.W for a subject of study or area of study	32
密	mì	形	secret	33
米	mǐ	量/名	meter; rice	40
面试	miànshì	名	interview	38
密码	mìmǎ	名	pin number, password	33
名列	mingliè	动	list as	33
模	mó	名	pattern	40
目	mù	名	list; eye	32
目录	mùlù	名	list, catalogue	32
目前	mùqián	副	at present	38
奶奶	nǎinai	名	grandma	34
难道	nándào	副	surely not, do you mean to say	37
内	nèi	名	inner	36
内部	nèibù	名	internal; interior	36
念	niàn	动	miss; study, read	34
年青人	niánqīng rén	名	young people	32
牛皮大王	niúpídàwáng	名	(colloquial) braggart	38
牛仔裤	niúzǎikù	名	jeans	39
暖气	nuǎnqì	名	central heating	39
女士	nǚshì	名	lady, madam	35
排	pái	动/名	put in order; row	33
排队	páiduì	动	queue	35
排行	páiháng	动/名	rank/ranking	33
乓 *	pāng	名	onomatopoeic character	32

袍子	páozi	名	robe	37
爬山	páshān	动	climbing a mountain, hiking	38
陪	péi	动	accompany	39
骗	piàn	动	cheat, deceive	39
聘	pìn	动	invite to engage	38
平	píng	形	even, level	35
乓*	pīng	名	onomatopoeic character	32
平方米	píngfāngmǐ	名	square metre	40
乒乓球	pīngpāngqiú	名	table tennis	32
平头	píngtóu	名	cropped hair	35
其	qí	代	that	39
齐	qí	形	full, complete	39
签	qiān	动	sign	36
千万	qiānwàn	副	absolutely, definitely, be sure to, must	39
起点	qǐdiǎn	名	starting point	31
切	qiè	动	be close to; cut	37
且	qiě		and; just	32
骑马	qímǎ	动	riding a horse	38
起名	qǐmíng	动+名	to name, to give name to	31
亲	qīn	名/动	next of kin; kiss	37
亲爱的	qīnàide	形	dear (intimate form of address); darling	37
请假	qǐngjià	动	ask for leave	36
请假条	qǐngjiàtiáo	名	written request for leave/absence	36
清真	qīngzhēn	名	Islamic, Muslim	31
齐全	qíquán	形	complete	39
求职信	qiúzhíxìn	名	job application letter	38
取	qǔ	动	get, take	31
区	qū		area, zone	36
全	quán	形	whole, complete	37
全部	quánbù	副/名	completely, all	37
区别	qūbié	名/动	difference	36
群	qún	名/量	cluster, group	40
染	rǎn	动	(to) colour	35

染发	rǎnfà	动+名	colour or dye hair	35
任	rèn	动	take a post	38
任何	rènhé	代	any	40
人民大会堂	Rénmín-dàhuìtáng	专名	The Great Hall of the People	40
人数	rénshù	名	number of people	31
热情	rèqíng	形/名	enthusiastic; zeal	38
日期	rìqī	名	date	37
融	róng	名	circulation	38
如	rú	连	if	31
如此	rúcǐ	副	be like this; so, such	37
如果	rúguǒ	连	if	31
商量	shāngliang	动	discuss, consult	32
商业	shāngyè	名	commercial; business	36
设	shè	动	set up	31
设备	shèbèi	名	facilities	31
设计	shèjì	动	design	35
神	shén	名	spirit; god	35
身	shēn	名	body	32
身份	shēnfèn	名	identity, status	33
身份证	shēnfènzhèng	名	ID card	33
胜	shèng		victory	38
胜任	shèngrèn	动	capable of, up to the job	38
身体	shēntǐ	名	body	32
申通	Shēntōng	专名	STO Express Co	34
匙*	shi	名	key	31
食	shí	名/动	food; eat	37
实	shí	形	actual, real	38
士	shì	名	person	35
世	shì	名	world	37
世界	shìjiè	名	world	37
食物	shíwù	名	food	37
实习	shíxí	动/名	do intern work; work experience	38
事先	shìxiān	副	beforehand; in advance	36

实习生	shíxíshēng	名	intern	38
使用	shǐyòng	动	utilise; use	33
市中心	shìzhōngxīn	名	city centre	35
熟	shóu	形	cooked; ripe	36
手工	shǒugōng	名	handmade; handwork	34
收获	shōuhuò	名/动	gains, harvest	37
手续	shǒuxù	名	procedure	31
数	shù	名	number	31
术	shù	名	art, technique	32
束	shù	动	tie, control	40
属	shǔ	动	be born in the year of, belong to	34
输	shū	动	transport; lose	34
刷	shuā	名/动	brush	39
帅	shuài	形	smart; handsome	35
帅哥	shuàigē	名	handsome man	39
书法	shūfǎ	名	calligraphy	32
睡衣	shuìyī	名	pyjama	34
书面	shūmiàn	形	written	36
顺	Shùn	介	along	34
顺丰	Shùnfēng	专名	SF Express	34
熟悉	shúxī	动/形	be familiar with	38
属相	shǔxiàng	名	signs of the Chinese zodiac	34
数学	shùxué	名	maths	31
死	sǐ	形/动	to death; dead, die	32
思	sī	动	thought, think	31
私	sī	形	private, personal	32
四联美发厅	Sìlián měifàtīng	专名	Silian Hairdressing	35
死期	sǐqī	名	fixed term (deposit account)	33
死去活来	sǐqùhuólái	短语	hovering between life and death, very much	39
私人	sīrén	形	private, personal	32
诉	sù	动	tell	36
苏	sū	动/名	revive; a surname	38

苏格兰	Sūgélán	专名	Scotland	38
随	suí	动	follow	39
随便	suíbiàn	副/形	casually, casual; as you like	39
所	suǒ	助	archaic written expression with no specific meaning, often omitted nowadays	40
所在	suǒzài	名	place; place where something exists	40
堂	táng	名	hall	40
烫	tàng	动	scald, burn	35
烫发	tàngfà	动+名	perm one's hair	35
淘	táo	动	wash	39
套	tào	名	cover; (量) a set of	34
淘宝	Táobǎo	专名	Taobao, Chinese online shopping website	39
替	tì	动/介	substitute; on behalf of	36
体	tǐ	名	body	32
天安门	Tiān'ānmén	专名	Tian'anmen	40
天帝	tiāndì	名	celestial emperor (Emperor of Heaven)	40
天猫	Tiānmāo	专名	Tmall, Chinese online shopping website	39
天文学	tiānwénxué	名	astronomy	40
调	tiáo	动	adjust	31
条件	tiáojiàn	名	conditions	37
提供	tígōng	动	provide	35
停止	tíngzhǐ	动	stop	40
同	tóng	形	same, similar	35
通告	tōnggào	名	public notice, announcement	36
通票	tōngpiào	名	multiple-venue ticket	40
同学	tóngxué	名	classmate, schoolmate	37
同志	tóngzhì	名	comrade	40
通知	tōngzhī	名/动	notice; notify	36
通知书	tōngzhīshū	名	(information) letter, notification	31
透	tòu	动/形	permeate; transparent	33
透支	tòuzhī	动	overdraft	33
退	tuì	动	send back, return, retreat	37
推	tuī	动	push	38
推销	tuīxiāo	动	promote; market	38

外宾	wàibīn	名	foreign guest	40
外资	wàizī	名	foreign investment	34
万	wàn	数	ten thousand	34
往	wǎng	介	toward	33
王小明	Wáng Xiǎomíng	专名	a Chinese name	31
王府井	Wángfǔjǐng	专名	a shopping street in Beijing	35
往来账户	wǎngláizhànghù	名	current account	33
万国邮联	Wànguó yóulián	专名	Universal Postal Union (UPU)	34
为	wéi	动	be; become	31
围	wéi	名	all round	36
微	wēi	形	small, tiny	40
位于	wèiyú	动	situated at/in	35
文科	wénkē	名	humanities	31
误	wù	名	error	37
武	wǔ	名	military	32
物美价廉	wùměijiàlián	短语	(product) cheap but good	39
武术	wǔshù	名	martial arts	32
误以为	wùyǐwéi	动	mistaken for; mistakenly believe	37
席	xí	名	seat	40
悉	xī	动	know	38
显	xiǎn	动	reveal, show	35
现成	xiànchéng	形	ready-made, off the shelf	36
现存	xiàncún	动	currently existing, surviving	40
香	xiāng	形	fragrant	33
相	xiāng		each other	34
相差	xiāngchà	动	differ from each other	34
相反	xiāngfǎn	形	opposite, contrary	37
香港	Xiānggǎng	专名	Hong Kong	33
相同	xiāngtóng	形	the same	36
相应	xiāngyìng	形	corresponding	35
香皂	xiāngzào	名	toilet soap	39
先进	xiānjìn	形	advanced	31
显眼	xiǎnyǎn	形	conspicuous	35

销	xiāo	动	sale	38
校队	xiàoduì	名	school/college team	32
校园	xiàoyuán	名	campus	31
西单	Xīdān	专名	a shopping street in Beijing	35
习惯	xíguàn	动/名	get used to; habit	37
系列	xìliè	名	series; serial	33
信封	xìnfēng	名	envelope	37
型	xíng	名	type	34
型	xíng	名	style, model	35
新鲜	xīnxiān	形	fresh	36
信箱	xìnxiāng	名	mailbox	38
信用	xìnyòng	名	credit	33
信用卡	xìnyòngkǎ	名	credit card	33
绣	xiù	动	embroider	34
修	xiū	动	repair; study	31
绣花	xiùhuā	动+名	embroidery	34
续	xù	动	continue	31
须	xū	情动	must	39
选	xuǎn	动	select	32
选修	xuǎnxiū	动/名	select an optional course	32
学历	xuélì	名	educational background	38
学名	xuémíng	名	scientific name, formal name	32
学生会	xuéshēnghuì	名	student union	36
学生证	xuéshēngzhèng	名	student card	32
学位	xuéwèi	名	(academic) degree	31
学习	xuéxí	动/名	study	31
牙膏	yágāo	名	toothpaste	39
宴	yàn	名	formal meal, banquet	40
阳	yáng	名	sun; masculine	34
羊	yáng	名	goat, sheep	36
阳历	yánglì	名	solar calendar; Gregory calendar	34
羊毛	yángmáo	名	wool	39
羊肉串	yángròu chuàn	名	lamb skewer	36

宴会	yànhuì	名	banquet	40
钥*	yào		key	31
钥匙	yàoshi	名	keys	31
牙刷	yáshuā	名	toothbrush	39
业务	yèwù	名	business, professional work	34
姨	yí	名	aunt	39
仪	yí	名	ceremony; appearance	40
意	yì	名	desire	38
以(……能力)	yǐ …nénglì	介	with (…the ability of)	38
一般	yìbān	副/形	common; generally	31
一开始	yìkāishǐ	副	at the beginning	37
引	yǐn	动	guide	35
因而	yīnér	连	thus, therefore	40
阴历	yīnlì	名	Chinese lunar calendar	34
银联	Yínlián	专名	UnionPay	33
引起	yǐnqǐ	动	cause, give rise to	35
一切	yíqiè	代	everything, all	37
仪式	yíshì	名	rite, ceremony	40
意思	yìsi	名	meaning	31
由	yóu	介	by	34
邮	yóu	名	post	34
优	yōu	形	exellent	39
优惠价	yōuhuìjià	名	preferential/special price	39
邮票	yóupiào	名	stamp	34
有意思	yǒuyìsi	动/形	be interesting	31
有意者	yǒuyìzhě	名	person who is interested	38
于	yú	介	at, in; a surname	35
与	yǔ	连	with	39
于爱华	Yú'àihuá	专名	a Chinese name	37
元	yuán	名	unit	33
原	yuán		original	34
元	yuán	名	element, component	37
原来	yuánlái	副	in fact, actually, originally	34

原因	yuányīn	名	cause, reason	36
语调	yǔdiào	名	intonation	37
预订	yùdìng	动	book (a place, ticket etc.) in advance	31
阅	yuè	动	read	31
约	yuē	副	about	31
月份	yuèfèn	名	month	34
阅览室	yuèlǎnshì	名	reading room	31
运	yùn	动	transport	34
运输	yùnshū	名/动	transport	34
与其……不如	yǔqí...bùrú	连	rather…than…	39
语音	yǔyīn	名	pronunciation; voice	37
预约	yùyuē	动/名	reserve; reservation	35
邮局	yóujú	名	post office	34
杂	zá	形	mixed	31
仔	zǎi	名	cub; child	39
皂	zào	名	soap	39
杂志	zázhì	名	magazine, journal	31
占	zhàn	动	occupy	40
占地	zhàndì	动	occupy an area of	40
账	zhàng	名	account	33
账户	zhànghù	名	account	33
招	zhāo	动	recruit; attract	38
招聘	zhāopìn	动	recruit	38
折	zhé	名/动	discount; fold, break	39
者	zhě	名	person	38
政	zhèng	名	certain administrative aspects of government	34
证	zhèng	名	certificate, card; proof	32
正式	zhèngshì	形	formal	36
真龙天子	zhēnlóngtiānzǐ	名	real son of the dragon (emperor)	40
职	zhí	名	profession	33
志	zhì	名	records	31
至	zhì	介	to	38
志	zhì	名	ideal, will	40

址	zhǐ	名	site	33
止	zhǐ	动	stop	40
之	zhī		of; object substitute	35
支付宝	Zhīfùbǎo	专名	Alipay	39
至今	zhìjīn	副	up to now	38
之一	zhīyī		one of	35
职员	zhíyuán	名	staff member	33
众	zhòng	名	mass	38
中国邮政	Zhōngguó yóuzhèng	专名	China Post	34
中文系	zhōngwénxì	名	department of Chinese language and literature	31
重要	zhòngyào	形	important	32
中天	zhōngtiān	名	centre of the cosmos	40
注	zhù	动	record, register	31
祝	zhù	动	wish	37
筑	zhù	动	construct	38
主	zhǔ		main, owner	40
装	zhuāng	动	put; hold	39
注册	zhùcè	动/名	register	31
住处	zhùchù	名	dwelling	33
追	zhuī	动	court; chase, pursue	39
准	zhǔn	动	allow	36
准假	zhǔnjià	动	authorize leave or absence	36
准时	zhǔnshí	形	on time	34
主修	zhǔxiū	动	major in	38
注意	zhùyì	动/名	pay attention; attention, notice	35
资	zī	名	capital	34
自动	zìdòng	形	automatic	32
自己	zìjǐ	代	oneself	36
紫禁城	Zǐjìnchéng	专名	Forbidden City	40
自觉	zìjué	形	conscious	32
紫微星	zǐwēixīng	专名	North Star	40
字样	zìyàng	名	written expressions	36
自由市场	zìyóushìchǎng	名	free market	39

总理	zǒnglǐ	名	premier, prime minister	40
走神	zǒushén	动	be distracted or absent minded, not concentrating	39
尊	zūn	动	respect	36
尊敬	zūnjìng	形/动	Dear (addressing letter); respected	36
伦敦欧洲商学院		专名	European Business School London	38
老王卖瓜，自卖自夸			boast of one's own trumpet	38

附录五　Appendix 5

英汉词汇表　English-Chinese Vocabulary List

英文	中文	拼音	词性	课号
a great quantity, a large number	大量	dàliàng	副	31
a Chinese name	李健	Lǐ Jiàn	专名	31
a Chinese name	于爱华	Yúàihuá	专名	37
a Chinese name	王小明	Wáng Xiǎomíng	专名	31
a phrase-final particle (fusion of 了 + 啊)	啦	la	助	37
a shopping street in Beijing	东单	Dōngdān	专名	35
a shopping street in Beijing	西单	Xīdān	专名	35
a shopping street in Beijing	王府井	Wángfǔjǐng	专名	35
a well known brand of steamed bun in Tianjin	狗不理包子	Gǒubùlǐbāozi	专名	37
ab initio; from scratch (starting from zero)	零起点	língqǐdiǎn	名	31
about	关于	guānyú	介	36
about	约	yuē	副	31
absolutely, definitely, be sure to, must	千万	qiānwàn	副	39
accompany	陪	péi	动	39
account	账	zhàng	名	33
account	账户	zhànghù	名	33
actual, real	实	shí	形	38
add, attach	附	fù	动	37
address	地址	dìzhǐ	名	33
adjust	调	tiáo	动	31
admission; admit (on a programme)	录取	lùqǔ	动/名	31
advanced	先进	xiānjìn	形	31
advertisement	广告	guǎnggào	名	36
ah	哎	āi	感叹	36
air conditioner	空调	kōngtiáo	名	31
Alipay	支付宝	Zhīfùbǎo	专名	39
all round	围	wéi	名	36

all, complete	俱	jù	形	32
allow	准	zhǔn	动	36
along	顺	Shùn	介	34
alongside; keep to; rely on	靠	kào	介/动	37
American Express	美国运通	Měiguó yùntōng	专名	33
ancient	古	gǔ	形	40
ancient times	古代	gǔdài	名	40
and; but also	而且	érqiě	连	32
and; just	且	qiě		32
any	任何	rènhé	代	40
approximately	大约	dàyuē	副	31
Arab, Arabic	阿拉伯	Ālābó	专名	37
archaic written expression with no specific meaning, often omitted nowadays	所	suǒ	助	40
architecture, construction	建筑	jiànzhù	名	38
area, zone	区	qū		36
arrive late	迟到	chídào	动	32
arrive; arrivals	到达	dàodá	动/名	34
art, technique	术	shù	名	32
ask for leave	请假	qǐngjià	动	36
astronomy	天文学	tiānwénxué	名	40
at present	目前	mùqián	副	38
at that time (year)	当年	dāngnián	名	34
at the beginning	一开始	yìkāishǐ	副	37
at, in; a surname	于	yú	介	35
attach	附上	fùshàng	动	37
aunt	姨	yí	名	39
aunt, term of address for a woman similar in age to one's parents	阿姨	āyí	名	39
authorize leave or absence	准假	zhǔnjià	动	36
automatic	自动	zìdòng	形	32
banquet	宴会	yànhuì	名	40
barber	理发师	lǐfàshī	名	35

baseball	棒球	bàngqiú	名	32
bat, stick; terrific (colloquial)	棒	bàng	名/形	32
be born in the year of, belong to	属	shǔ	动	34
be called as	称为	chēngwéi	动	40
be close to; cut	切	qiè	动	37
be distracted or absent minded, not concentrating	走神	zǒushén	动	39
be familiar with	熟悉	shúxī	动/形	38
be hospitable	好客	hàokè	形	37
be interesting	有意思	yǒuyìsi	动/形	31
be like this; so, such	如此	rúcǐ	副	37
be proficient in	精通	jīngtōng	动/形	38
be seated, take one's seat	就座	jiùzuò	动	36
be; become	为	wéi	动	31
beautician	美容师	měiróng shī	名	35
beautiful woman	美女	měinǚ	名	39
become	成为	chéngwéi	动	33
become one's turns; turn, wheel	轮	lún	动/名	35
bed sheet	床单	chuángdān	名	34
beforehand; in advance	事先	shìxiān	副	36
benefit	惠	huì	动	39
besides, in addition	另外	lìngwài	副	33
black bear; a coward	狗熊	gǒuxióng	名	39
blow dry	吹	chuī	动	35
boast of one's own trumpet	老王卖瓜, 自卖自夸			38
boast; praise	夸	kuā	动	38
body	身	shēn	名	32
body	身体	shēntǐ	名	32
body	体	tǐ	名	32
book (a place, ticket etc.) in advance	预订	yùdìng	动	31
border, boundary	际	jì	名	33

(colloquial) braggart	牛皮大王	niúpídàwáng	名	38
branch	分行	fēnháng	名	38
branch; subject	科	kē	名	31
broadway; avenue	大街	dàjiē	名	35
browse	览	lǎn	动	31
brush	刷	shuā	名/动	39
build	建	jiàn	动	38
bunch	串	chuàn	名	36
bureau	局	jú	名	34
business, professional work	业务	yèwù	名	34
but	而	ér		32
by	由	yóu	介	34
calendar	历法	lìfǎ	名	34
call; say	称	chēng	动	40
calligraphy	书法	shūfǎ	名	32
campus	校园	xiàoyuán	名	31
capable of, up to the job	胜任	shèngrèn	动	38
capacity; quantity	量	liàng	名	31
capital	资	zī	名	34
capture, reap	获	huò	动	37
card	卡	kǎ	名	32
casually, casual; as you like	随便	suíbiàn	副/形	39
cause, give rise to	引起	yǐnqǐ	动	35
cause, reason	原因	yuányīn	名	36
celestial emperor (Emperor of Heaven)	天帝	tiāndì	名	40
central heating	暖气	nuǎnqì	名	39
centre of the cosmos	中天	zhōngtiān	名	40
ceremony; appearance	仪	yí	名	40
certain administrative aspects of government	政	zhèng	名	34
certificate, card; proof	证	zhèng	名	32
Chairman Mao	毛主席	Máozhǔxí	专名	40

change	改变	gǎibiàn	动	32
change, correct	改	gǎi	动	32
change; alter	更改	gēnggǎi	动	33
chat	聊	liáo	动	32
chat	聊天	liáotiān	动	32
cheap	廉	lián	形	39
(product) cheap but good	物美价廉	wùměijiàlián	短语	39
cheat, deceive	骗	piàn	动	39
China Post	中国邮政	Zhōngguó yóuzhèng	专名	34
Chinese as a foreign language	对外汉语	duìwài hànyǔ	名	31
Chinese lunar calendar	阴历	yīnlì	名	34
circles; boundary	界	jiè	名	37
circulation	融	róng	名	38
city centre	市中心	shìzhōngxīn	名	35
classmate, schoolmate	同学	tóngxué	名	37
clever	聪	cōng	形	36
climbing a mountain, hiking	爬山	páshān	动	38
club	俱乐部	jùlèbù	名	32
cluster of buildings	建筑群	jiànzhùqún	名	40
cluster, group	群	qún	名/量	40
coach, trainer	教练	jiàoliàn	名	32
(to) colour	染	rǎn	动	35
colour or dye hair	染发	rǎnfà	动+名	35
come from	来自	láizì	动	31
come on a visit	来访	láifǎng	动	40
commemorate	纪念	jìniàn	名/动	34
commercial; business	商业	shāngyè	名	36
commodity, goods	货	huò	名	33
common; generally	一般	yìbān	副/形	31
companion	伴	bàn	名	37
compared with; comparably	较	jiào	副	33

complete	毕	bì	动	38
complete	齐全	qíquán	形	39
completely, all	全部	quánbù	副/名	37
comrade	同志	tóngzhì	名	40
conditions	条件	tiáojiàn	名	37
conduct, carry out	进行	jìnxíng	动	31
connect	联	lián	动	33
conscious	自觉	zìjué	形	32
conspicuous	显眼	xiǎnyǎn	形	35
construct	筑	zhù	动	38
contact	联系	liánxì	动	33
continue	续	xù	动	31
convenient	方便	fāngbiàn	形	32
conversation	会话	huìhuà	名	31
cooked; ripe	熟	shóu	形	36
copy	抄	chāo	动	36
corresponding	相应	xiāngyìng	形	35
cosmetology; improve one's looks	美容	měiróng	动+名	35
court; chase, pursue	追	zhuī	动	39
cover; (量) a set of	套	tào	名	34
credit	信用	xìnyòng	名	33
credit card	信用卡	xìnyòngkǎ	名	33
cropped hair	平头	píngtóu	名	35
cub; child	仔	zǎi	名	39
currency	货币	huòbì	名	33
current (account)	活期	huóqī	名	33
current account	往来账户	wǎngláizhànghù	名	33
currently existing, surviving	现存	xiàncún	动	40
customer	顾客	gùkè	名	35
cut	剪	jiǎn	动	35
cut and blow (hair)	连剪带吹	liánjiǎndàichuī		35
date	日期	rìqī	名	37

English	Chinese	Pinyin	Type	Lesson
deal with, process	办理	bànlǐ	动	31
Dear (addressing letter); respected	尊敬	zūnjìng	形/动	36
dear (intimate form of address); darling	亲爱的	qīnàide	形	37
debit card	借记卡	jièjìkǎ	名	33
(academic) degree	学位	xuéwèi	名	31
department of Chinese language and literature	中文系	zhōngwénxì	名	31
department store	百货大楼	bǎihuòdàlóu	名	39
department, part, section	部	bù	名	32
deposit; store	存	cún	动	33
design	设计	shèjì	动	35
desire	意	yì	名	38
differ from each other	相差	xiāngchà	动	34
difference	区别	qūbié	名/动	36
different	不同	bùtóng	形	35
discount; fold, break	折	zhé	名/动	39
discuss, consult	商量	shāngliang	动	32
diversified	多元	duōyuán	形	37
do intern work; work experience	实习	shíxí	动/名	38
do, handle	办	bàn	动	31
dress	连衣裙	liányīqún	名	39
dwelling	住处	zhùchù	名	33
each other	相	xiāng		34
educational background	学历	xuélì	名	38
element, component	元	yuán	名	37
embarrassed; sorry	不好意思	bùhǎoyìsi	短语	32
embezzle	盗用	dàoyòng	动	33
embroider	绣	xiù	动	34
embroidery	绣花	xiùhuā	动+名	34
emperor	皇	huáng	名	38
emperor	皇帝	huángdì	名	40
emperor, imperial	帝	dì	名	40
engage in advanced studies	进修	jìnxiū	动	31

English	中文	Pinyin	词性	页
engaged in (for a job)	从事	cóngshì	动	34
enthusiastic; zeal	热情	rèqíng	形/名	38
envelope	信封	xìnfēng	名	37
error	误	wù	名	37
especially, exceptionally	格外	géwài	副	40
European Business School London	伦敦欧洲商学院		专名	38
even more	更加	gèngjiā	副	36
even, level	平	píng	形	35
every, each	每	měi	代	31
everything, all	一切	yíqiè	代	37
exaggerating; exaggerate	夸张	kuāzhāng	形/动	38
example	例子	lìzi	名	36
exception	例外	lìwài	名	37
exellent	优	yōu	形	39
exercise; activity	活动	huódòng	动/名	32
experience	经历	jīnglì	名/动	38
express delivery	快递	kuàidì	名	34
express; expression	表达	biǎodá	动/名	37
external	对外	duìwài	介宾结构	36
facilities	设备	shèbèi	名	31
fat	肥	féi	形	39
fax	传真	chuánzhēn	名	38
feature (of the face)	脸型	liǎnxíng	名	35
finance	金融	jīnróng	名	38
finish, end	结束	jiéshù	动	40
fixed term	定期	dìngqī	名	33
fixed term (deposit account)	死期	sǐqī	名	33
floor; layer	层	céng	量	36
follow	随	suí	动	39
food	食物	shíwù	名	37
food; eat	食	shí	名/动	37

for example	比如	bǐrú	动	34
forbid	禁	jìn	动	40
forbid	禁止	jìnzhǐ	动	40
Forbidden City	紫禁城	Zǐjìnchéng	专名	40
forbidden place	禁地	jìndì	名	40
foreign guest	外宾	wàibīn	名	40
foreign investment	外资	wàizī	名	34
forge	锻	duàn	动	32
formal	正式	zhèngshì	形	36
formal meal, banquet	宴	yàn	名	40
format	格式	géshì	名	37
forms	表格	biǎogé	名	31
fragrant	香	xiāng	形	33
free market	自由市场	zìyóushìchǎng	名	39
fresh	新鲜	xīnxiān	形	36
full, complete	齐	qí	形	39
gains, harvest	收获	shōuhuò	名/动	37
get a job; employment	就业	jiùyè	动/名	36
get used to; habit	习惯	xíguàn	动/名	37
get, take	取	qǔ	动	31
give discount	打折	dǎzhé	动	39
give lecture, teach	讲课	jiǎngkè	动	37
glamour	华	huá	名	38
goat, sheep	羊	yáng	名	36
graduate	毕业	bìyè	动	38
grandma	奶奶	nǎinai	名	34
guest	宾	bīn	名	35
guide	引	yǐn	动	35
gym	健身房	jiànshēnfáng	名	32
habitation; live	居住	jūzhù	名/动	37
hair	发	fà	名	35
hair style	发型	fàxíng	名	35

English	Chinese	Pinyin	Part of Speech	Page
hairdressing salon	理发店	lǐfàdiàn	名	35
hall	堂	táng	名	40
hand over	递	dì	动	34
handmade; handwork	手工	shǒugōng	名	34
handsome man	帅哥	shuàigē	名	39
harbour	港	gǎng	名	33
have diarrhoea	拉肚子	lādùzi	动	36
have one's hair styled	美发	měifà	动+名	35
healthy	康	kāng	形	37
healthy	健*	jiàn	形	31
healthy; health	健康	jiànkāng	形/名	37
hobby	爱好	àihào	名/动	38
hold up	举	jǔ	动	40
hold, take place	举行	jǔxíng	动	40
hole	洞	dòng	名	39
Hong Kong	香港	Xiānggǎng	专名	33
Hong Kong dollar	港币	gǎngbì	专名	33
honour	敬	jìng		36
hot pot	火锅	huǒguō	名	37
hovering between life and death, very much	死去活来	sǐqùhuólái	短语	39
humanities	文科	wénkē	名	31
hurriedly	连忙	liánmáng	副	39
Hyde (transliteration)	海德	Hǎidé	专名	38
ID card	身份证	shēnfènzhèng	名	33
ideal, will	志	zhì	名	40
identity, status	身份	shēnfèn	名	33
if	如	rú	连	31
if	如果	rúguǒ	连	31
important	重要	zhòngyào	形	32
in fact, actually, originally	原来	yuánlái	副	34
inner	内	nèi	名	36
instance	例	lì	名	36

intelligent, clever	聪明	cōngming	形	36
intentionally	故意	gùyì	副	39
intentionally; cause; old	故	gù	副/名/形	39
interest (financial)	利息	lìxi	名	33
intern	实习生	shíxíshēng	名	38
internal	对内	duìnèi	介宾结构	36
internal; interior	内部	nèibù	名	36
international	国际	guójì	名	33
interview	面试	miànshì	名	38
intonation	语调	yǔdiào	名	37
intonation, tone	调	diào	名	37
invite to engage	聘	pìn	动	38
Islamic, Muslim	清真	qīngzhēn	名	31
jeans	牛仔裤	niúzǎikù	名	39
Jingdong, Chinese online shopping website	京东	Jīngdōng	专名	39
job application letter	求职信	qiúzhíxìn	名	38
karaoke	卡拉OK	kǎlā ok	名	38
keep fit	健身	jiànshēn	名/动	32
key	匙*	shi	名	31
key	钥*	yào		31
keys	钥匙	yàoshi	名	31
know	悉	xī	动	38
lady, madam	女士	nǚshì	名	35
lamb skewer	羊肉串	yángròu chuàn	名	36
large size	大型	dàxíng	形	34
late	迟	chí	形	32
lecture	讲座	jiǎngzuò	名	36
(information) letter, notification	通知书	tōngzhīshū	名	31
like, love	好	hào	动	37
limits	范	fàn		36
list as	名列	míngliè	动	33

list, catalogue	目录	mùlù	名	32
list; eye	目	mù	名	32
live	居	jū	动	37
live; alive	活	huó	动/形	32
long established brand (shop)	老字号	lǎozìhào	名	35
long skirt	长裙	chángqún	名	39
long woollen underpants	毛裤	máokù	名	39
look after	顾	gù	动	35
look, observe	观	guān	动	40
lose	丢	diū	动	33
M.W for a subject of study or area of study	门	mén	量	32
magazine, journal	杂志	zázhì	名	31
mailbox	信箱	xìnxiāng	名	38
main, owner	主	zhǔ		40
major in	主修	zhǔxiū	动	38
Malaysia	马来西亚	Mǎláixīyà	专名	31
manage; management	管理	guǎnlǐ	动/名	34
manner; approach	方式	fāngshì	名	32
mansion	府	fǔ	名	35
mark	标	biāo	名/动	33
mark	标记	biāojì	名	33
martial arts	武术	wǔshù	名	32
mass	众	zhòng	名	38
mate	伙	huǒ	名	37
maths	数学	shùxué	名	31
meaning	意思	yìsi	名	31
Meibai Hairdressing	美白美发厅	Měibái měifàtīng	专名	35
membership card	会员卡	huìyuán kǎ	名	32
memorial hall	纪念堂	jìniàntáng	名	40
meter; rice	米	mǐ	量/名	40
method	方法	fāngfǎ	名	36

military	武	wǔ	名	32
mind; manage	管	guǎn	动	33
mini skirt	超短裙	chāoduǎnqún	名	39
minor in	副修	fùxiū	动	38
miss; study, read	念	niàn	动	34
mistake, error	错误	cuòwù	名	37
mistaken for; mistakenly believe	误以为	wùyǐwéi	动	37
mixed	杂	zá	形	31
month	月份	yuèfèn	名	34
most	大部分	dàbùfen	名	32
multiple-venue ticket	通票	tōngpiào	名	40
museum	博物馆	bówùguǎn	名	40
must	必须	bìxū	情动	39
must	须	xū	情动	39
necessity; necessary	必要	bìyào	名/形	39
next of kin; kiss	亲	qīn	名/动	37
no matter	不管	bùguǎn	连	33
North Star	紫微星	zǐwēixīng	专名	40
not necessarily	不见得	bújiànde	副	37
not only	不仅	bùjǐn	连	32
not only…but also…	不仅……而且……	bùjǐn...érqiě		32
notice; notify	通知	tōngzhī	名/动	36
noun prefix	阿	ā	助	37
number	数	shù	名	31
number of people	人数	rénshù	名	31
occupy	占	zhàn	动	40
occupy an area of	占地	zhàndì	动	40
of; object substitute	之	zhī		35
office	办公室	bàngōngshì	名	31
old	故	gù	形	40

old; used (not for age)	旧	jiù	形	33
on the spot, there and then	当场	dāngchǎng	形副	39
on time	准时	zhǔnshí	形	34
one of	之一	zhīyī		35
oneself	己	jǐ	代	36
oneself	自己	zìjǐ	代	36
only	仅	jǐn	副	32
onomatopoeic character	乓*	pāng	名	32
onomatopoeic character	乒*	pīng	名	32
opposite, contrary	相反	xiāngfǎn	形	37
opposite; against	反	fǎn	形	37
or	或，或者	huò/huòzhě	连	34
oral	口头	kǒutóu	形	36
orchid	兰	lán	名	38
original	原	yuán		34
other, another	另	lìng	形	33
otherwise, if not	不然	bùrán	连	31
outstanding	出色	chūsè	形	35
outstanding	出众	chūzhòng	形	38
overdraft	透支	tòuzhī	动	33
palace	宫	gōng	名	40
parcel	包裹	bāoguǒ	名	34
partner	伙伴	huǒbàn	名	37
pass on	传	chuán	动	38
paste	膏	gāo	名	39
pattern	模	mó	名	40
pay attention; attention, notice	注意	zhùyì	动/名	35
pay fees	交费	jiāofèi	动+名	31
peace	安	ān	名	40
perfect; accuracy	精	jīng	形/名	38
period, session	节	jié	量	32

perm one's hair	烫发	tàngfà	动+名	35
permeate; transparent	透	tòu	动/形	33
person	士	shì	名	35
person	者	zhě	名	38
person who is interested	有意者	yǒuyìzhě	名	38
pin number, password	密码	mìmǎ	名	33
place; department	处	chù	名	33
place; place where something exists	所在	suǒzài	名	40
plaits	辫	biàn	名	37
plaits, pigtail	辫子	biànzi	名	37
post	邮	yóu	名	34
post office	邮局	yóujú	名	34
pot	锅	guō	名	37
preferential/special price	优惠价	yōuhuìjià	名	39
premier, prime minister	总理	zǒnglǐ	名	40
preserve	保存	bǎocún	动	40
pressing	急	jí	形	34
price	价格	jiàgé	名	34
private, personal	私	sī	形	32
private, personal	私人	sīrén	形	32
procedure	手续	shǒuxù	名	31
profession	职	zhí	名	33
promote; market	推销	tuīxiāo	动	38
pronunciation; voice	语音	yǔyīn	名	37
provide	提供	tígōng	动	35
public notice, announcement	通告	tōnggào	名	36
publicize	公开	gōngkāi	动	36
pull; defecate	拉	lā	动	36
purchase	购	gòu	动	39
push	推	tuī	动	38
put in order; row	排	pái	动/名	33
put; hold	装	zhuāng	动	39

English	Chinese	Pinyin	POS	Lesson
pyjama	睡衣	shuìyī	名	34
queue	排队	páiduì	动	35
quilt	被	bèi	名	34
quilt cover	被套	bèitào	名	34
rank	列	liè	名/动	33
rank/ranking	排行	páiháng	动/名	33
rather…than…	与其……不如	yǔqí…bùrú	连	39
reach	达	dá	动	34
read	阅	yuè	动	31
read; study (a subject)	读	dú	动	31
reading room	阅览室	yuèlǎnshì	名	31
ready-made, off the shelf	现成	xiànchéng	形	36
real son of the dragon (emperor)	真龙天子	zhēnlóngtiānzǐ	名	40
record, register	注	zhù	动	31
records	志	zhì	名	31
recruit	招聘	zhāopìn	动	38
recruit; attract	招	zhāo	动	38
refine	炼	liàn	动	32
register	注册	zhùcè	动/名	31
relatively; compare	比较	bǐjiào	副/动	33
repair;study	修	xiū	动	31
report one's arrival or presence	报到	bàodào	动	31
reserve; reservation	预约	yùyuē	动/名	35
respect	尊	zūn	动	36
rest assure of	放心	fàngxīn	动	33
reveal, show	显	xiǎn	动	35
revive; a surname	苏	sū	动/名	38
reward	奖	jiǎng	名	33
riding a horse	骑马	qímǎ	动	38
risk	风险	fēngxiǎn	名	38
rite, ceremony	仪式	yíshì	名	40
robe	袍子	páozi	名	37

English	Chinese	Pinyin	POS	Page
royal family	皇家	huángjiā	名	38
royal palace	皇宫	huánggōng	名	40
rule	规	guī	名/动	40
safe	保险	bǎoxiǎn	形	34
salary	工资	gōngzī	名	38
sale	销	xiāo	动	38
salute; yours sincerely(ending letter), extend greetings	敬礼	jìnglǐ	动	36
same, similar	同	tóng	形	35
scald, burn	烫	tàng	动	35
scale	规模	guīmó	名	40
scene	景	jǐng	名	40
scholarship	奖学金	jiǎngxuéjīn	名	33
school/college team	校队	xiàoduì	名	32
science (subjects of study)	理科	lǐkē	名	31
scientific name, formal name	学名	xuémíng	名	32
scope, range	范围	fànwéi	名	36
Scotland	苏格兰	Sūgélán	专名	38
seal; m.w for letter	封	fēng	动/量	37
seat	席	xí	名	40
secondary; deputy, vice	副	fù	形	38
secret	密	mì	形	33
seem, like	好像	hǎoxiàng	副	36
select	选	xuǎn	动	32
select an optional course	选修	xuǎnxiū	动/名	32
send back, return, retreat	退	tuì	动	37
series; serial	系列	xìliè	名	33
set up	设	shè	动	31
set up, offer	开设	kāishè	动	31
settle accounts	结算	jiésuàn	动	33
SF Express	顺丰	Shùnfēng	专名	34
share	份	fèn	名	33

sheet	单	dān	名	34
(go) shopping; shopping	购物	gòuwù	动+名	39
short	短	duǎn	形	35
sign	签	qiān	动	36
signs of the Chinese zodiac	属相	shǔxiàng	名	34
Silian Hairdressing	四联美发厅	Sìlián měifàtīng	专名	35
single; bill	单	dān	形/名	33
site	址	zhǐ	名	33
situated at/in	位于	wèiyú	动	35
skill	技	jì	名	38
skill	技能	jìnéng	名	38
sky; air	空	kōng	名	34
small, tiny	微	wēi	形	40
smart	精	jīng	形	35
smart looking, lively	精神	jīngshén	形/名	35
smart; handsome	帅	shuài	形	35
soap	肥皂	féizào	名	39
soap	皂	zào	名	39
solar calendar; Gregory calendar	阳历	yánglì	名	34
spend winter, go through winter	过冬	guòdōng	动	39
spirit; god	神	shén	名	35
spoil; be used to	惯	guàn	动	37
spoon	匙*	chí	名	31
square formed by cross lines; check	格	gé	名	31
square metre	平方米	píngfāngmǐ	名	40
staff member	职员	zhíyuán	名	33
stamp	邮票	yóupiào	名	34
start/open (a business)	开业	kāiyè	动	35
starting point	起点	qǐdiǎn	名	31
steal	盗	dào	动	33
steamship	轮船	lúnchuán	名	34
STO Express Co	申通	Shēntōng	专名	34

stop	停止	tíngzhǐ	动	40
stop	止	zhǐ	动	40
(city) square	广场	guǎngchǎng	名	32
street	街	jiē	名	35
strength	力量	lìliàng	名	31
strenuous, require great effort	吃力	chīlì	形	37
student card	学生证	xuéshēngzhèng	名	32
student union	学生会	xuéshēnghuì	名	36
study	学习	xuéxí	动/名	31
stupid, slow	笨	bèn	形	36
style of cooking, cuisine	菜系	càixì	名	31
style, model	型	xíng	名	35
substitute; on behalf of	替	tì	动/介	36
sun; masculine	阳	yáng	名	34
supermarket	超市	chāoshì	名	33
supply	供	gōng	动	35
surely not, do you mean to say	难道	nándào	副	37
swear at, curse	骂	mà	动	39
table tennis	乒乓球	pīngpāngqiú	名	32
take a post	任	rèn	动	38
take physical exercise	锻炼	duànliàn	动	32
talent	才	cái	名	38
talent	才华	cáihuá	名	38
talk	讲	jiǎng	动	36
Taobao, Chinese online shopping website	淘宝	Táobǎo	专名	39
team	队	duì	名	32
team member	队员	duìyuán	名	32
tell	告	gào	动	36
tell	告诉	gàosù	动	36
tell	诉	sù	动	36
ten thousand	万	wàn	数	34
that	其	qí	代	39

English	汉字	Pinyin	词性	课
The Forbidden City	故宫	gùgōng	专名	40
The Great Hall of the People	人民大会堂	Rénmíndàhuìtáng	专名	40
the same	相同	xiāngtóng	形	36
thought, think	思	sī	动	31
thus, therefore	因而	yīnér	连	40
Tian'anmen	天安门	Tiān'ānmén	专名	40
tie, control	束	shù	动	40
tight	紧	jǐn	形	34
Tmall, Chinese online shopping website	天猫	Tiānmāo	专名	39
to	至	zhì	介	38
to death; dead, die	死	sǐ	形/动	32
to name, to give name to	起名	qǐmíng	动+名	31
toilet soap	香皂	xiāngzào	名	39
toothbrush	牙刷	yáshuā	名	39
toothpaste	牙膏	yágāo	名	39
tourist spot	景点	jǐngdiǎn	名	40
toward	往	wǎng	介	33
transform	改造	gǎizào	动	35
transport	运	yùn	动	34
transport	运输	yùnshū	名/动	34
transport by air, airmail	空运	kōngyùn	名	34
transport by sea, surface mail	海运	hǎiyùn	名	34
transport; lose	输	shū	动	34
treasure	宝	bǎo	名	39
type	型	xíng	名	34
type; like	般	bān	助	31
ultimately, in the end, after all	到底	dàodǐ	副	34
uncle	伯	bó	名	37
unexpectedly	居然	jūrán	副	38
UnionPay	银联	Yínlián	专名	33
unit	单位	dānwèi	名	36
unit	元	yuán	名	33

English	Chinese	Pinyin	Type	Page
unit; module	单元	dānyuán	名	33
Universal Postal Union (UPU)	万国邮联	Wànguó yóulián	专名	34
unlined trousers; single layer of outer trousers	单裤	dānkù	名	39
up to now	至今	zhìjīn	副	38
urgent, emergency	紧急	jǐnjí	形	34
utilise; use	使用	shǐyòng	动	33
value, price	价	jià	名	34
various	多种多样	duōzhǒng duōyàng	形	33
vast, extensive	博	bó	形	40
victory	胜	shèng		38
VIP	贵宾	guìbīn	名	35
visit	访	fǎng	动	40
visit and tour around (a place)	参观	cānguān	动	40
volume, book	册	cè	名	31
walk around (shops), ramble, stroll	逛	guàng	动	39
wash	淘	táo	动	39
well	井	jǐng	名	35
wheel	轮	lún	名	34
which	何	hé	名	40
whole, complete	全	quán	形	37
will, about to, be going to	将	jiāng	副	36
wish	祝	zhù	动	37
with	与	yǔ	连	39
with (…the ability of)	以 (……能力)	yǐ …nénglì	介	38
wool	羊毛	yángmáo	名	39
world	世	shì	名	37
world	世界	shìjiè	名	37
worry about; miss	挂念	guàniàn	动	37
wrap	裹	guǒ	名/动	34
written	书面	shūmiàn	形	36
written expressions	字样	zìyàng	名	36
written request for leave/absence	请假条	qǐngjiàtiáo	名	36
young people	年青人	niánqīng rén	名	32